THE COLLECTED POEMS

AMY LEVY

The Collected Poems

EMPYREAN SERIES · SUBLUNARY EDITIONS · SEATTLE, WA

EMPYREAN SERIES No. 30

about   This volume includes the entirety of *A London Plane-Tree and Other Verse* (London: T. Fisher Unwin, 1889) and *A Minor Poet and Other Verse* (2nd edition. London: T. Fisher Unwin, 1891), as well as a few other poems absent from those volumes.

isbn   978-1-955190-50-3

CONTENTS

Note on the Text

The following collection is presented chronologically, as best we can surmise. We have relied heavily on the bibliographies compiled by scholars like Melvyn New and, in particular, Linda Hunt Beckman; we owe a great debt of gratitude to them both. We have also been fortunate enough to locate a poem and series of translations that have, thus far, escaped cataloguing: the original poem "In Switzerland" and a few fragments of the Romanian poet Carmen Sylva.

Introduction[1]

Oscar Wilde

The gifted subject of these paragraphs, whose distressing death has brought sorrow to many who knew her only from her writings, was born at Clapham and spent the greater part of her short and outwardly uneventful life in Clapham. Her family was Jewish, but she herself, as she grew up, gradually ceased to hold the orthodox doctrines of her nation, retaining, however, a strong race feeling. At a very early age she showed a marked turn for writing, and some of her childish verses, still preserved, are both correct and original. During the years 1880 and 1881 she was a student at Newnham College, Cambridge, and while still in residence published her first volume of verse, *Xantippe*. The modest little paper-covered book, which contains only thirty pages, was published in Cambridge, and was, we believe, never advertised. Its merit, however, attracted a good deal of attention, and the whole edition was sold out. "Xantippe", the longest and most important poem, had been written three years earlier, and had already appeared (in May, 1880) in the *University Magazine*. Xantippe on her death-bed relates the disappointment of her life, beginning with her love for her husband, and her longing to share his thoughts:—

---

1. This piece was originally published shortly after Levy's suicide in November of 1889. It appeared in the Wilde-edited *Woman's World*, Vol. 3.

> I, guided by his wisdom and his love,
> Led by his words and counselled by his care,
> Should lift the shrouding vale from things which be,
> And at the flowing fountain of his soul
> Refresh my thirsting spirit...

But Socrates wanted no such companion or disciple in his wife, and gradually her love turned to bitterness:—

> Then faded that vain fury; hope died out;
> A huge despair was stealing on my soul,
> A sort of fierce acceptance of my fate—
> He wished a household vessel—well! 'twas good
> For he should have it! ...
>   ...till at last I grew
> As ye have known me,—eye exact to mark
> The texture of the spinning; ear all keen
> For aimless talking when the moon is up,
> And ye should be a-sleeping; tongue to cut
> With quick incision, 'thwart the merry words
> Of idle maidens...

This poem—surely a most remarkable one to be produced by a girl still at school—is distinguished, as nearly all Miss Levy's work is, by the qualities of sincerity, directness, and melancholy. In expression it is less simple and lucid than some of her later verse, far less so for instance, than the two short poems which we publish in this issue; but its spirit is the same, and no intelligent critic could fail to see the promise of greater things.

A Minor Poet, and Other Verse, published in 1884, showed a distinct advance. This, too, is but a thin volume, with no single superfluous line in it. The two epitaphs with which it closes, and the dedication "to a dead poet" with which it opens, are perhaps the most perfect and complete things in it; these, if they stood alone, would be enough to mark their writer as a poet of no mean excellence.

A third volume of poems was nearly ready for publication at the time of her death, and is to appear immediately. Some of the pieces to be included in it have appeared already in various papers and magazines, and two or three of these are among her very best work.

Her prose work consists almost entirely of fiction. The few magazine articles which she wrote are good of their kind, but they lack that special individuality which makes the value of her other writing. Of her short stories, two or three are slight and careless, written from a very superficial stratum of thought or feeling, and produced with the utmost facility. Of these stories she herself was the first to speak slightingly, and she would never have sanctioned their republication. But even these are marked by a strong vitality. They are careless, but not dull; they show how much the touch of the real artist tells, even in second-rate work. But besides these there a few other short stories which are by no means second-rate. Among those may be named "Cohen of Trinity", "Eldorado at Islington", "Addenbroke", "Wise in Her Generation" — one of her latest, which we give in our present number — and "The Recent Telepathic

Occurrence at the British Museum".[2] This last is a good example of Miss Levy's extraordinary power of condensation. The story occupied only about a page of this magazine, and it gives the whole history of a wasted and misunderstood love. There is not so much as a name in it, but the relation of the man and woman stands out vivid as if we had known and watched its growth.

Miss Levy's two novels, *The Romance of a Shop* and *Reuben Sachs*, were both published last year. The first is a bright and clever story, full of sparkling touches; the second is a novel that probably no other writer could have produced. Its directness, its uncompromising truth, its depth of feeling, and, above all, its absence of any single superfluous word, make it, in some sort, a classic. Like all her best work it is sad, but the sadness is by no means morbid. The strong undertone of moral earnestness, never preached, gives a stability and force to the vivid portraiture, and prevents the satiric touches from degenerating into mere malice. Truly the book is an achievement.

To write thus at six-and-twenty is given to very few; and from the few thus endowed their readers may safely hope for yet greater things later on. But "later on" has not come for the writer of *Reuben Sachs*, and the world must forego the full fruition of her power. The loss is the world's, but perhaps not hers. She was never robust; not often actually ill, but seldom well enough to feel life a joy instead of a burden; and her work

2. Available online at https://sublunaryeditions.com/blog/ the-recent-telepathic-occurrence-at-the-british-museum-amy-levy

was not poured out lightly, but drawn drop by drop from the very depth of her own feeling. We may say of it that it was in truth her life's blood.

The Collected Poems

The Ballad of Ida Grey

A Story of Woman's Sacrifice

The nightingale sang tenderly,
In the gentle evening breeze,
As a knight and maiden saunter'd
(Arm-in-arm) beneath the trees,
She was clad in samite snowy;
He, in dazzling armour bright,
And their voices murmur'd softly
In the shadow of the night.
"Ida Grey," (the man quoth sadly)
"Thou whose heart is link'd with mine,
And who lov'st, with such a fondness,
This too hasty knight of thine;
Thy pure soul will shrink in horror,
Thy young love will change to hate,
When thou hearest the dread story
Which I will to thee relate.
Thou know'st well my kinsman Siegfried,
In the glory of youth's prime,
That to-morrow he will suffer
For a foul and bloody crime;—

1. Part II was never published, as *The Pelican* folded after its second issue.

That with sounds of shame and horror
The indignant nations ring;—
Ida, Ida, he is bloodless,
It was I that slew the king!
In a moment of mad passion,
When my brain with wine was hot,
He had mocked me, and I slew him,
Aye, I slew him on the spot!
Then, in guilty, guilty terror,
From the palace-hall I fled;
And I left him (noble Siegfried!)
To support the blame instead.
Ida Grey! my life's at peril,
Death may come,—and with death hell!
And now, ere I fly my country,
I have come to bid 'farewell'."
When the knight had finish'd speaking,
There was silence for a space;
Then, retreating further from him,
She look'd up into his face.
Seem'd her voice like rolling thunder,
Burnt her eye with angry flame:
"I renounce thee now for ever!
Go! weak heart, confess thy shame."
Heaved her bosom with emotion,
Stood a tear within her eye;
Then, in mournful tones, she added,
"But thou art not fit to die!

Thou, so wicked and so bloodstain'd;
Death is only for the good.
Lo! to shrive thee, will I give thee,
Knight! mine own chaste maidenhood!"

Run to Death

A True Incident of Pre-Revolutionary French History

Now the lovely autumn morning breathes its freshness
    in earth's face,
In the crowned castle courtyard the blithe horn proclaims
    the chase;
And the ladies on the terrace smile adieux with rosy lips
To the huntsmen disappearing down the cedar-shaded groves,
Wafting delicate aromas from their scented finger tips,
And the gallants wave in answer, with their gold-embroidered
    gloves.
On they rode, past bush and bramble, on they rode,
    past elm and oak;
And the hounds, with anxious nostril, sniffed the
    heather-scented air,
Till at last, within his stirrups, up Lord Gaston rose, and spoke—
He, the boldest and the bravest of the wealthy nobles there:
"Friends," quoth he, "the time hangs heavy,
    for it is not as we thought,
And these woods, tho' fair and shady, will afford, I fear, no sport.
Shall we hence, then, worthy kinsmen, and desert the hunter's
    track
For the chateau, where the wine cup and the dice cup tempt
    us back?"

"Ay," the nobles shout in chorus; "Ay," the powder'd
   lacquey cries;
Then they stop with eager movement, reining in quite
   suddenly;
Peering down with half contemptuous, half with wonder-
   opened eyes
At a "something" which is crawling, with slow step, from
   tree to tree.
Is't some shadow phantom ghastly? No, a woman and a child,
Swarthy woman, with the "gipsy" written clear upon her face;
Gazing round her with her wide eyes dark, and shadow-fringed,
   and wild,
With the cowed suspicious glances of a persecuted race.
Then they all, with unasked question, in each other's faces peer,
For a common thought has struck them, one their lips dare
   scarcely say,—
Till Lord Gaston cries, impatient, "Why regret the stately deer
When such sport as yonder offers? quick! unleash the dogs
   —away!"
Then they breath'd a shout of cheering, grey-haired man
   and stripling boy,
And the gipsy, roused to terror, stayed her step, and turned her
   head—
Saw the faces of those huntsmen, lit with keenest cruel joy—
Sent a cry of grief to Heaven, closer clasped her child, and fled!

*
* *

O ye nobles of the palace! O ye gallant-hearted lords!
Who would stoop for Leila's kerchief, or for Clementina's
      gloves,
Who would rise up all indignant, with your shining
      sheathless swords,
At the breathing of dishonour to your languid lady loves!
O, I tell you, daring nobles, with your beauty-loving stare,
Who ne'er long the coy coquetting of the courtly
      dames withstood,
Tho' a woman be the lowest, and the basest, and least fair,
In your manliness forget not to respect her womanhood,
And thou, gipsy, that hast often the pursuer fled before,
That hast felt ere this the shadow of dark death upon thy brow,
That hast hid among the mountains, that hast roamed
      the forest o'er,
Bred to hiding, watching, fleeing, may thy speed avail thee now!

* *
* *

Still she flees, and ever fiercer tear the hungry hounds behind,
Still she flees, and ever faster follow there the huntsmen on,
Still she flees, her black hair streaming in a fury to the wind,
Still she flees, tho' all the glimmer of a happy hope is gone.
"Eh? what? baffled by a woman! Ah, sapristi! she can run!
Should she 'scape us, it would crown us with dishonour
      and disgrace;
It is time" (Lord Gaston shouted) "such a paltry chase
      were done!"

And the fleeter grew her footsteps, so the hotter grew
    the chase —
Ha! at last! the dogs are on her! will she struggle ere she dies?
See! she holds her child above her, all forgetful of her pain,
While a hundred thousand curses shoot out darkly
    from her eyes,
And a hundred thousand glances of the bitterest disdain.
Ha! the dogs are pressing closer! they have flung her
    to the ground;
Yet her proud lips never open with the dying sinner's cry —
Till at last, unto the Heavens, just two fearful shrieks resound,
When the soul is all forgotten in the body's agony!
Let them rest there, child and mother, in the shadow of the oak,
On the tender mother-bosom of that earth from which
    they came.
As they slow rode back those huntsmen neither laughed,
    nor sang, nor spoke,
Hap, there lurked unowned within them throbbings of
    a secret shame.
But before the flow'ry terrace, where the ladies smiling sat,
With their graceful nothings trifling all the weary time away,
Low Lord Gaston bowed, and raising high his richly
    'broider'd hat,
"Fairest ladies, give us welcome! 'Twas a famous hunt to-day."

Xantippe

A Fragment

What, have I waked again? I never thought
To see the rosy dawn, or ev'n this grey,
Dull, solemn stillness, ere the dawn has come.
The lamp burns low; low burns the lamp of life:
The still morn stays expectant, and my soul,
All weighted with a passive wonderment,
Waiteth and watcheth, waiteth for the dawn.
Come hither, maids; too soundly have ye slept
That should have watched me; nay, I would not chide —
Oft have I chidden, yet I would not chide
In this last hour;—now all should be at peace.
I have been dreaming in a troubled sleep
Of weary days I thought not to recall;
Of stormy days, whose storms are hushed long since;
Of gladsome days, of sunny days; alas!
In dreaming, all their sunshine seem'd so sad,
As though the current of the dark To-Be
Had flow'd, prophetic, through the happy hours.
And yet, full well, I know it was not thus;
I mind me sweetly of the summer days,
When, leaning from the lattice, I have caught
The fair, far glimpses of a shining sea;

And, nearer, of tall ships which thronged the bay,
And stood out blackly from a tender sky
All flecked with sulphur, azure, and bright gold;
And in the still, clear air have heard the hum
Of distant voices; and methinks there rose
No darker fount to mar or stain the joy
Which sprang ecstatic in my maiden breast
Than just those vague desires, those hopes and fears,
Those eager longings, strong, though undefined,
Whose very sadness makes them seem so sweet.
What cared I for the merry mockeries
Of other maidens sitting at the loom?
Or for sharp voices, bidding me return
To maiden labour? Were we not apart,—
I and my high thoughts, and my golden dreams,
My soul which yearned for knowledge, for a tongue
That should proclaim the stately mysteries
Of this fair world, and of the holy gods?
Then followed days of sadness, as I grew
To learn my woman-mind had gone astray,
And I was sinning in those very thoughts—
For maidens, mark, such are not woman's thoughts—
(And yet, 'tis strange, the gods who fashion us
Have given us such promptings)...

                           Fled the years,
Till seventeen had found me tall and strong,
And fairer, runs it, than Athenian maids
Are wont to seem; I had not learnt it well—

My lesson of dumb patience — and I stood
At Life's great threshold with a beating heart,
And soul resolved to conquer and attain...
Once, walking 'thwart the crowded market place,
With other maidens, bearing in the twigs
White doves for Aphrodite's sacrifice,
I saw him, all ungainly and uncouth,
Yet many gathered round to hear his words,
Tall youths and stranger-maidens — Sokrates —
I saw his face and marked it, half with awe,
Half with a quick repulsion at the shape...
The richest gem lies hidden furthest down,
And is the dearer for the weary search;
We grasp the shining shells which strew the shore,
Yet swift we fling them from us; but the gem
We keep for aye and cherish. So a soul,
Found after weary searching in the flesh
Which half repelled our senses, is more dear,
For that same seeking, than the sunny mind
Which lavish Nature marks with thousand hints
Upon a brow of beauty. We are prone
To overweigh such subtle hints, then deem,
In after disappointment, we are fooled...
And when, at length, my father told me all,
That I should wed me with great Sokrates,
I, foolish, wept to see at once cast down
The maiden image of a future love,
Where perfect body matched the perfect soul.

But slowly, softly did I cease to weep;
Slowly I 'gan to mark the magic flash
Leap to the eyes, to watch the sudden smile
Break round the mouth, and linger in the eyes;
To listen for the voice's lightest tone —
Great voice, whose cunning modulations seemed
Like to the notes of some sweet instrument.
So did I reach and strain, until at last
I caught the soul athwart the grosser flesh.
Again of thee, sweet Hope, my spirit dreamed!
I, guided by his wisdom and his love,
Led by his words, and counselled by his care,
Should lift the shrouding veil from things which be,
And at the flowing fountain of his soul
Refresh my thirsting spirit...

                          And indeed,
In those long days which followed that strange day
When rites and song, and sacrifice and flow'rs,
Proclaimed that we were wedded, did I learn,
In sooth, a-many lessons; bitter ones
Which sorrow taught me, and not love inspired,
Which deeper knowledge of my kind impressed
With dark insistence on reluctant brain; —
But that great wisdom, deeper, which dispels
Narrowed conclusions of a half-grown mind,
And sees athwart the littleness of life
Nature's divineness and her harmony,
Was never poor Xantippe's...

                    I would pause
And would recall no more, no more of life,
Than just the incomplete, imperfect dream
Of early summers, with their light and shade,
Their blossom-hopes, whose fruit was never ripe;
But something strong within me, some sad chord
Which loudly echoes to the later life,
Me to unfold the after-misery
Urges with plaintive wailing in my heart.
Yet, maidens, mark; I would not that ye thought
I blame my lord departed, for he meant
No evil, so I take it, to his wife.
'Twas only that the high philosopher,
Pregnant with noble theories and great thoughts,
Deigned not to stoop to touch so slight a thing
As the fine fabric of a woman's brain—
So subtle as a passionate woman's soul.
I think, if he had stooped a little, and cared,
I might have risen nearer to his height,
And not lain shattered, neither fit for use
As goodly household vessel, nor for that
Far finer thing which I had hoped to be…
Death, holding high his retrospective lamp,
Shows me those first, far years of wedded life,
Ere I had learnt to grasp the barren shape
Of what the Fates had destined for my life.
Then, as all youthful spirits are, was I
Wholly incredulous that Nature meant

So little, who had promised me so much.
At first I fought my fate with gentle words,
With high endeavours after greater things;
Striving to win the soul of Sokrates,
Like some slight bird, who sings her burning love
To human master, till at length she finds
Her tender language wholly misconceived,
And that same hand whose kind caress she sought,
With fingers flippant flings the careless corn…
I do remember how, one summer's eve,
He, seated in an arbour's leafy shade,
Had bade me bring fresh wine-skins…

                              As I stood
Ling'ring upon the threshold, half concealed
By tender foliage, and my spirit light
With draughts of sunny weather, did I mark
An instant, the gay group before mine eyes.
Deepest in shade, and facing where I stood,
Sat Plato, with his calm face and low brows
Which met above the narrow Grecian eyes,
The pale, thin lips just parted to the smile,
Which dimpled that smooth olive of his cheek.
His head a little bent, sat Sokrates,
With one swart finger raised admonishing,
And on the air were borne his changing tones.
Low lounging at his feet, one fair arm thrown
Around his knee (the other, high in air
Brandish'd a brazen amphor, which yet rained

Bright drops of ruby on the golden locks
And temples with their fillets of the vine),
Lay Alkibiades the beautiful.
And thus, with solemn tone, spake Sokrates:
"This fair Aspasia, which our Perikles
Hath brought from realms afar, and set on high
In our Athenian city, hath a mind,
I doubt not, of a strength beyond her race;
And makes employ of it, beyond the way
Of women nobly gifted: woman's frail—
Her body rarely stands the test of soul;
She grows intoxicate with knowledge; throws
The laws of custom, order, 'neath her feet,
Feasting at life's great banquet with wide throat."
Then sudden, stepping from my leafy screen,
Holding the swelling wine-skin o'er my head,
With breast that heaved, and eyes and cheeks aflame,
Lit by a fury and a thought, I spake:
"By all great powers around us! can it be
That we poor women are empirical?
That gods who fashioned us did strive to make
Beings too fine, too subtly delicate,
With sense that thrilled response to ev'ry touch
Of nature's, and their task is not complete?
That they have sent their half-completed work
To bleed and quiver here upon the earth?
To bleed and quiver, and to weep and weep,
To beat its soul against the marble walls

Of men's cold hearts, and then at last to sin!"
I ceased, the first hot passion stayed and stemmed
And frighted by the silence: I could see,
Framed by the arbour foliage, which the sun
In setting softly gilded with rich gold,
Those upturned faces, and those placid limbs;
Saw Plato's narrow eyes and niggard mouth,
Which half did smile and half did criticise,
One hand held up, the shapely fingers framed
To gesture of entreaty—"Hush, I pray,
Do not disturb her; let us hear the rest;
Follow her mood, for here's another phase
Of your black-browed Xantippe…"

                              Then I saw
Young Alkibiades, with laughing lips
And half-shut eyes, contemptuous shrugging up
Soft, snowy shoulders, till he brought the gold
Of flowing ringlets round about his breasts.
But Sokrates, all slow and solemnly,
Raised, calm, his face to mine, and sudden spake:
"I thank thee for the wisdom which thy lips
Have thus let fall among us: prythee tell
From what high source, from what philosophies
Didst cull the sapient notion of thy words?"
Then stood I straight and silent for a breath,
Dumb, crushed with all that weight of cold contempt;
But swiftly in my bosom there uprose
A sudden flame, a merciful fury sent

To save me; with both angry hands I flung
The skin upon the marble, where it lay
Spouting red rills and fountains on the white;
Then, all unheeding faces, voices, eyes,
I fled across the threshold, hair unbound—
White garment stained to redness—beating heart
Flooded with all the flowing tide of hopes
Which once had gushed out golden, now sent back
Swift to their sources, never more to rise...
I think I could have borne the weary life,
The narrow life within the narrow walls,
If he had loved me; but he kept his love
For this Athenian city and her sons;
And, haply, for some stranger-woman, bold
With freedom, thought, and glib philosophy...
Ah me! the long, long weeping through the nights,
The weary watching for the pale-eyed dawn
Which only brought fresh grieving: then I grew
Fiercer, and cursed from out my inmost heart
The Fates which marked me an Athenian maid.
Then faded that vain fury; hope died out;
A huge despair was stealing on my soul,
A sort of fierce acceptance of my fate,—
He wished a household vessel—well! 'twas good,
For he should have it! He should have no more
The yearning treasure of a woman's love,
But just the baser treasure which he sought.
I called my maidens, ordered out the loom,

And spun unceasing from the morn till eve;
Watching all keenly over warp and woof,
Weighing the white wool with a jealous hand.
I spun until, methinks, I spun away
The soul from out my body, the high thoughts
From out my spirit; till at last I grew
As ye have known me, — eye exact to mark
The texture of the spinning; ear all keen
For aimless talking when the moon is up,
And ye should be a-sleeping; tongue to cut
With quick incision, 'thwart the merry words
Of idle maidens...

     Only yesterday
My hands did cease from spinning; I have wrought
My dreary duties, patient till the last.
The gods reward me! Nay, I will not tell
The after years of sorrow; wretched strife
With grimmest foes — sad Want and Poverty; —
Nor yet the time of horror, when they bore
My husband from the threshold; nay, nor when
The subtle weed had wrought its deadly work.
Alas! alas! I was not there to soothe
The last great moment; never any thought
Of her that loved him — save at least the charge,
All earthly, that her body should not starve...
You weep, you weep; I would not that ye wept;
Such tears are idle; with the young, such grief
Soon grows to gratulation, as, "her love

Was withered by misfortune; mine shall grow
All nurtured by the loving," or, "her life
Was wrecked and shattered—mine shall smoothly sail."
Enough, enough. In vain, in vain, in vain!
The gods forgive me! Sorely have I sinned
In all my life. A fairer fate befall
You all that stand there…

                    Ha! the dawn has come;
I see a rosy glimmer—nay! it grows dark;
Why stand ye so in silence? throw it wide,
The casement, quick; why tarry?—give me air—
O fling it wide, I say, and give me light!

The Shepherd

From Goethe

There was an idle shepherd, fond of sleep
Who never troubled him about his sheep.

But by a maiden was he captive led —
He left the bottle, sleep and hunger fled.

His passion drove him to unrest and flight;
He'd moan and groan and count the stars at night!

*   *   *   *

But when, at length, the maiden he had ta'en,
Sleep, hunger, thirst — they all came back again.

A Fragment[1]

The sad rain falls from Heaven,
    A sad bird pipes and sings;
I am sitting here at my window
    And watching the spires of King's.

O fairest of all fair places,
    Sweetest of all sweet towns!
With the birds, and the greyness and greenness,
    And the men in caps and gowns.

All they that dwell within thee,
    To leave are ever loth,
For one man gets friends, and another
    Gets honour, and one gets both.

The sad rain falls from Heaven;
    My heart is great with woe —
I have neither a friend nor honour,
    Yet I am sorry to go.

---

1. First appeared as "Imitation of Heine" in *Cambridge Review*, December 7, 1881. It was reprinted under the current title in *A Minor Poet and Other Verse*.

A Prayer

Since that I may not have
Love on this side the grave,
 Let me imagine Love.
Since not mine is the bliss
Of "claspt hands and lips that kiss,"
 Let me in dreams it prove.
What tho' as the years roll
No soul shall melt to my soul,
 Let me conceive such thing;
Tho' never shall entwine
Loving arms around mine
 Let dreams caresses bring.
To live—it is my doom—
Lonely as in a tomb,
 This cross on me was laid;
My God, I know not why;
Here in the dark I lie,
 Lonely, yet not afraid.
It has seemed good to Thee
Still to withhold the key
 Which opes the way to men;
I am shut in alone,
I make not any moan,
 Thy ways are past my ken.

Yet grant me this, to find
The sweetness in my mind
    Which I must still forego;
Great God which art above,
Grant me to image Love,—
    The bliss without the woe.

Ralph to Mary

Love, you have led me to the strand,
    Here, where the stilly, sunset sea,
    Ever receding silently,
Lays bare a shining stretch of sand;

Which, as we tread, in waving line,
    Sinks softly 'neath our moving feet;
    And looking down our glances meet,
Two mirrored figures—yours and mine.

To-night you found me sad, alone,
    Amid the noisy, empty books
    And drew me forth with those sweet looks,
And gentle ways which are your own.

The glory of the setting sun
    Has sway'd and softened all my mood;
    This wayward heart you understood,
Dear love, as you have always done.

Have you forgot the poet wild,
    Who sang rebellious songs and hurl'd
    His fierce anathemas at "the world,"
Which shrugg'd its shoulders, pass'd and smil'd?

Who fled in wrath to distant lands,
        And sitting, thron'd upon a steep,
        Made music to the mighty deep,
And thought, "Perhaps it understands."

Who back return'd, a wanderer drear,
        Urged by the spirit's restless pain,
        Sang his wild melodies in vain—
Sang them to ears that would not hear...

A weary, lonely thing he flies,
        His soul's fire with soul's hunger quell'd,
        Till, sudden turning, he beheld
His meaning—mirrored in your eyes!...

Ah, Love, since then have passed away
        Long years; some things are chang'd on earth;
        Men say that poet had his worth,
And twine for him the tardy bay.

What care I, so that hand in hand,
        And heart in heart we pace the shore?
        My heart desireth nothing more,
We understand,—we understand.

"Felo de Se"

With Apologies to Mr. Swinburne.

For repose I have sighed and have struggled; have sigh'd
    and have struggled in vain;
I am held in the Circle of Being and caught in the
    Circle of Pain.
I was wan and weary with life; my sick soul yearned for death;
I was weary of women and war and the sea and the wind's
    wild breath;
I cull'd sweet poppies and crush'd them, the blood ran
    rich and red:—
And I cast it in crystal chalice and drank of it till I was dead.
And the mould of the man was mute, pulseless in ev'ry part,
The long limbs lay on the sand with an eagle eating the heart.
Repose for the rotting head and peace for the putrid breast,
But for that which is "I" indeed the gods have decreed no rest;
No rest but an endless aching, a sorrow which grows amain:—
I am caught in the Circle of Being and held in the
    Circle of Pain.
Bitter indeed is Life, and bitter of Life the breath,
But give me Life and its ways and its men, if this be Death.
Wearied I once of the Sun and the voices which
    clamour'd around:
Give them me back—in the sightless depths there is neither
    light nor sound.

Sick is my soul, and sad and feeble and faint as it felt
When (far, dim day) in the fair flesh-fane of the body it dwelt.
But then I could run to the shore, weeping and weary
    and weak;
See the waves' blue sheen and feel the breath of the breeze
    on my cheek:
Could wail with the wailing wind; strike sharply the hands
    in despair;
Could shriek with the shrieking blast, grow frenzied and
    tear the hair;
Could fight fierce fights with the foe or clutch at
    a human hand;
And weary could lie at length on the soft, sweet, saffron sand…
I have neither a voice nor hands, nor any friend nor a foe; I am
I—just a Pulse of Pain—I am I, that is all I know.
For Life, and the sickness of Life, and Death and
    desire to die; —
They have passed away like the smoke, here is nothing but
    Pain and I.

Sonnet

Most wonderful and strange it seems, that I
Who but a little time ago was tost
High on the waves of passion and of pain,
With aching heat and wildly throbbing brain,
Who peered into the darkness, deeming vain
All things there found if but One thing were lost,
Thus calm and still and silent here should lie,
Watching and waiting,—waiting passively.

The dark has faded, and before mine eyes
Have long, grey flats expanded, dim and bare;
And through the changing guises all things wear
Inevitable Law I recognise:
Yet in my heart a hint of feeling lies
Which half a hope and half is a despair.

Translated from Geibel

O Say, thou wild, thou oft deceived heart,
What mean these noisy throbbings in my breast?
After thy long, unutterable woe
    Wouldst thou not rest?

Fall'n from Life's tree the sweet rose-blossom lies,
And fragrant youth has fled. What made to seem
This earth as fair to thee as Paradise,
    Was all a dream.

The blossom fell, the thorn was left to me;
Deep from the wound the blood-drops ever flow,
All that I have are yearnings, wild desires,
    And wrath and woe.

They brought me Lethe's water, saying, "Drink!"
"Drink, for the draught is sweet," I heard them say,
"Shalt learn how soft a thing forgetting is."
    I answered: "Nay."

What tho' indeed it were an idle cheat,
Nathless to me 'twas very fair and blest:
With every breath I draw I know that love
    Reigns in my breast.

Let me go forth,—and thou, my heart, bleed on:
A lonely spot I seek by night and day,
That love and sorrow I may there breathe forth
        In a last lay.

From Grillparzer's *Sappho*[1]

PHAON

And who had thought that Hellas' highest maid
On Hellas' lowest youth would deign to glance?

SAPPHO

Fate and theyself thou wrong'st; forbear to scorn
The golden gifts which gods delight to pour
On cheek and brow, in heart and breast, at birth
Of one by them mark'd out for happiness.
A beauteous body is a beauteous gift,
Ay, and a priceless gem is joy of life:
The daring of bold men, the iron might
Of lords o' the earth, firm will; the strength to bear
That which the fates have destin'd, fantasy,
(A servant, a chaste handmaid as is meet)
These are the things which deck life's thorny way:—
Life's highest aim is, after all, to live.
Not vainly did the muses choose to bind
The barren laurel-leaf about their brows;
Upon his head, to whom it erst has giv'n
Fair promise of reward of sacrifice,

1. 1813 play by the Austrian playright Franz Grillparzer (1791–1872).

Cold, without fruit or fragrance, presses it.
Who stands aloft upon the topmost peaks
In suff'ring stands; poor Art is ever driv'n
To beg of Life's abundance.

ACT I

Sappho

O Phaon, Phaon, what did I to thee?
Peaceful I stood in the fair meads of song,
Alone, and made gold-stringed melody.
Earth's joy and gladness from on high I saw;
Earth's sorrows could not reach me. And I knew
The flight of Time, the God who never stays,
Not by the hours, but by the spotless blooms
Enwoven in the wreath of Poesy.
Eternal youth was green about my head,
And what I gave to song, song gave to me.
Then comes he, one rough man, and with rude hands
Tears down the golden veil before mine eyes,
Leads me below into the desert waste,
Where is no path nor any print of foot;
And now, the one light shining in the void,
He draws his hand from mine, woe's me! and flees.

ACT IV

From Heine[1]

My heart, my heart is heavy,
Yet May is bright in the land;
High up on the grey old rampart
'Neath the linden tree I stand.

Below, the moat round the city
Azure-waved, peacefully flows;
A lad in a boat glides onwards,
And fishes and sings as he goes.

Gay-hued, small in the distance,
To right and to left one sees
Houses and gardens and people,
Oxen and meadows and trees.

Women are bleaching linen,
They leap in the grass and bound;
The mill-wheel splashes diamonds,
I hear from afar the sound.

1. Translation of Heine's poem beginning "Mein Herz, mein Herz ist traurig"
from *Buch der Lieder* [Book of songs].

There stands by the old grey tower
A sentry box, small and low,
And the sentinel, red-coated,
Is pacing there to and fro.

With his gun he is playing;
It gleams in the sunlight's red;
Now he "presents" it;—now "shoulders"—
I wish he would shoot me dead.

The Sick Man in the Garden

From Lenau

So late, and yet a nightingale?
Long since have dropped the blossoms pale,
The summer fields are ripening,
       And yet a sound of spring?

O tell me, didst thou come to hear,
Sweet Spring, that I should die this year;
And call'st across from the far shore
       To me one greeting more?

To Death

From Lenau

If within my heart there's mould,
    If the flame of Poesy,
And the flame of Love grow cold,
    Slay my body utterly.

Swiftly, pause not nor delay;
    Let not my life's field be spread
With the ash of feelings dead,
    Let thy singer soar away.

The Ballad of Last Seeing

It is so very long ago,
    A little thing, I am aware;
I heard the music's ebb and flow,
    I raised my head and saw you there.
Cold was your face, as cold as fair,
    You did not stay to smile or greet;
Sunshines and music filled the air
    The last time that I saw you, sweet.

Beneath the arching portico
    Carved round about with carvings rare
You paused a space, then turned to go,
    I watched you down the sculptured stair.
I did not hear the organ's blare,
    Sole heard I your departing feet;
I cared so much, you did not care,
    The last time that I saw you, sweet.

Friend, if indeed it must be so,
    And we no more on earth may meet,
One time was dear to me I know—
    The last time that I saw you, sweet.

A Cross-Road Epitaph

"Am Kreuzweg wird begraben
Wer selber brachte sich um."

When first the world grew dark to me
I call'd on God, yet came not he.
Whereon, as wearier wax'd my lot,
On Love I call'd, but Love came not.
When a worse evil did befall,
Death, on thee only did I call.

Epitaph

On a Commonplace Person Who Died in Bed

This is the end of him, here he lies:
The dust in his throat, the worm in his eyes,
The mould in his mouth, the turf on his breast;
This is the end of him, this is best.
He will never lie on his couch awake,
Wide-eyed, tearless, till dim daybreak.
Never again will he smile and smile
When his heart is breaking all the while.
He will never stretch out his hands in vain
Groping and groping—never again.
Never ask for bread, get a stone instead,
Never pretend that the stone is bread.
Never sway and sway 'twixt the false and true,
Weighing and noting the long hours through.
Never ache and ache with the chok'd-up sighs;
This is the end of him, here he lies.

In the Black Forest[1]

I lay beneath the pine trees,
      And looked aloft, where, through
The dusky, clustered tree-tops,
      Gleamed rent, gay rifts of blue.

I shut my eyes, and a fancy
      Fluttered my sense around:
"I lie here dead and buried,
      And this is churchyard ground.

I am at rest for ever;
      Ended the stress and strife."
Straight I fell to and sorrowed
      For the pitiful past life.

Right wronged, and knowledge wasted;
      Wise labour spurned for ease;
The sloth and the sin and the failure;
      Did I grow sad for these?

They had made me sad so often;
      Not now they made me sad;
My heart was full of sorrow
      For joy it never had.

1. First published as "After Heine", *Cambridge Review*, December 3, 1884.
The title here is taken from *A London Plane-Tree and Other Verse* (1889)

Fragments of Carmen Sylva[1]

The fairest word on earth that's heard,
On human lips the fairest word,
      Is mother.
To whom such name shall once belong,
High honor hers her whole life long,
      A mother.
But all her earthly joys are o'er,
Who is and then who is no more
      A mother.

*   *   *   *

Ye, having heart and strength to bear
    Deep in the fervent-growing soul,
Whom the fierce flames of Passion's self
    But strengthen, making firm and whole.

Ye, having might, when tempests rage,
    To lift the head, free, fearing nought,
Whom the heart-pressing weight of life
    Rules with the sway of earnest thought;

1. Published as part of the article "Carmen Sylva, Queen of Roumania" by Helen Zimmern in *The Century Illustrated Monthly Magazine*, vol. 28, 1884.

Ye, breathing only light and warmth,
　　Forever, like a live sun's ray,
Till tenderly the bare black earth
　　Kindness and joy brings forth straightway;—

Smiling, great burdens have ye borne,
　　Mountains of woe, and still smile on;
Guerdonless, where not trumpets sound,
　　Victorious battles have ye won.

There laurel is not, nor loud fame;
　　There secret tear-drops fall like dew.
O Heroes, whom now crowds proclaim,
　　Women, I give this book to you.

In Switzerland

Above my head the sky is blue,
Matching the rippling lake in hue.
All round about the mountains rise,
A green delight to weary eyes.
Here, where the place is warm and fair,
Where soft moss grows, where all the air
Is sweet with pungent scent of pine,
Stretched, prone and passive, I recline.
Around me lie the books and rugs,
The basket, boiler, teapot, mugs,
And all the other things that we
Have carried up for work and tea.
Walled round with tomes of ponderous size,
Her pen the busy Ellen plies.
Kit Marlow is her theme. Enough
I've had of all your dead men's stuff.
Kit Marlow's dead since long ago,
And I'm alive to-day, I know.
Heigho! I kick my heels i' the sun!
What matter if the work's undone?
Give me the warm sweet air, the sound
That Nature whispers soft around,
The lights and shadows in the trees,
And let them write their books that please.

The Dream

Believe me, this was true last night,
Tho' it is false to-day.
A.M.F. ROBINSON.

A fair dream to my chamber flew:
Such a crowd of folk that stirred,
Jested, fluttered; only you,
You alone of all that band,
Calm and silent, spake no word.
Only once you neared my place,
And your hand one moment's space
Sought the fingers of my hand;
Your eyes flashed to mine; I knew
All was well between us two.

*　　　　*　　　　*　　　　*

On from dream to dream I past,
But the first sweet vision cast
Mystic radiance o'er the last.

*　　　　*　　　　*　　　　*

When I woke the pale night lay
Still, expectant of the day;

All about the chamber hung
Tender shade of twilight gloom;
The fair dream hovered round me, clung
To my thought like faint perfume:—
Like sweet odours, such as cling
To the void flask, which erst encloses
Attar of rose; or the pale string
Of amber which has lain with roses.

To a Dead Poet

I knew not if to laugh or weep;
    They sat and talked of you—
"'Twas here he sat; 'twas this he said!
    'Twas that he used to do.

"Here is the book wherein he read,
    The room wherein he dwelt;
And he" (they said) "was such a man,
    Such things he thought and felt."

I sat and sat, I did not stir;
    They talked and talked away.
I was as mute as any stone,
    I had no word to say.

They talked and talked; like to a stone
    My heart grew in my breast—
I, who had never seen your face
    Perhaps I knew you best.

A Minor Poet

What should such fellows as I do,
Crawling between earth and heaven?

Here is the phial; here I turn the key
Sharp in the lock. Click!—there's no doubt it turned.
This is the third time; there is luck in threes—
Queen Luck, that rules the world, befriend me now
And freely I'll forgive you many wrongs!
Just as the draught began to work, first time,
Tom Leigh, my friend (as friends go in the world),
Burst in, and drew the phial from my hand,
(Ah, Tom! ah, Tom! that was a sorry turn!)
And lectured me a lecture, all compact
Of neatest, newest phrases, freshly culled
From works of newest culture: "common good";
"The world's great harmonies; "must be content
With knowing God works all things for the best,
And Nature never stumbles." Then again,
"The common good", and still, "the common, good";
And what a small thing was our joy or grief
When weigh'd with that of thousands. Gentle Tom,
But you might wag your philosophic tongue
From morn till eve, and still the thing's the same:

I am myself, as each man is himself—
Feels his own pain, joys his own joy, and loves
With his own love, no other's. Friend, the world
Is but one man; one man is but the world.
And I am I, and you are Tom, that bleeds
When needles prick your flesh (mark, yours, not mine).
I must confess it; I can feel the pulse
A-beating at my heart, yet never knew
The throb of cosmic pulses. I lament
The death of youth's ideal in my heart;
And, to be honest, never yet rejoiced
In the world's progress—scarce, indeed, discerned;
(For still it seems that God's a Sisyphus
With the world for stone).

                    You shake your head. I'm base,
Ignoble? Who is noble—you or I?
I was not once thus? Ah, my friend, we are
As the Fates make us.

                This time is the third;
The second time the flask fell from my hand,
Its drowsy juices spilt upon the board;
And there my face fell flat, and all the life
Crept from my limbs, and hand and foot were bound
With mighty chains, subtle, intangible;
While still the mind held to its wonted use,
Or rather grew intense and keen with dread,
An awful dread—I thought I was in Hell.
In Hell, in Hell! Was ever Hell conceived

By mortal brain, by brain Divine devised,
Darker, more fraught with torment, than the world
For such as I? A creature maimed and marr'd
From very birth. A blot, a blur, a note
All out of tune in this world's instrument.
A base thing, yet not knowing to fulfil
Base functions. A high thing, yet all unmeet
For work that's high. A dweller on the earth,
Yet not content to dig with other men
Because of certain sudden sights and sounds
(Bars of broke music; furtive, fleeting glimpse
Of angel faces 'thwart the grating seen)
Perceived in Heaven. Yet when I approach
To catch the sound's completeness, to absorb
The faces' full perfection, Heaven's gate,
Which then had stood ajar, sudden falls to,
And I, a-shiver in the dark and cold,
Scarce hear afar the mocking tones of men:
"He would not dig, forsooth; but he must strive
For higher fruits than what our tillage yields;
Behold what comes, my brothers, of vain pride!"
Why play with figures? trifle prettily
With this my grief which very simply's said,
"There is no place for me in all the world"?
The world's a rock, and I will beat no more
A breast of flesh and blood against a rock...
A stride across the planks for old time's sake.
Ah, bare, small room that I have sorrowed in;

Ay, and on sunny days, haply, rejoiced;
We know some things together, you and I!
Hold there, you rangèd row of books! In vain
You beckon from your shelf. You've stood my friends
Where all things else were foes; yet now I'll turn
My back upon you, even as the world
Turns it on me. And yet—farewell, farewell!
You, lofty Shakespere, with the tattered leaves
And fathomless great heart, your binding's bruised
Yet did I love you less? Goethe, farewell;
Farewell, triumphant smile and tragic eyes,
And pitiless world-wisdom!

                For all men
These two. And 'tis farewell with you, my friends,
More dear because more near: Theokritus;
Heine that stings and smiles; Prometheus' bard;
(I've grown too coarse for Shelley latterly:)
And one wild singer of to-day, whose song
Is all aflame with passionate bard's blood
Lash'd into foam by pain and the world's wrong.
At least, he has a voice to cry his pain;
For him, no silent writhing in the dark,
No muttering of mute lips, no straining out
Of a weak throat a-choke with pent-up sound,
A-throb with pent-up passion...

                Ah, my sun!
That's you, then, at the window, looking in
To beam farewell on one who's loved you long

And very truly. Up, you creaking thing,
You squinting, cobwebbed casement!

                       So, at last,
I can drink in the sunlight. How it falls.
Across that endless sea of London roofs,
Weaving such golden wonders on the grey,
That almost, for the moment, we forget
The world of woe beneath them.

                         Underneath,
For all the sunset glory, Pain is king.
Yet, the sun's there, and very sweet withal;
And I'll not grumble that it's only sun,
But open wide my lips—thus—drink it in;
Turn up my face to the sweet evening sky
(What royal wealth of scarlet on the blue
So tender toned, you'd almost think it green)
And stretch my hands out—so—to grasp it tight.
Ha, ha! 'tis sweet awhile to cheat the Fates,
And be as happy as another man.
The sun works in my veins like wine, like wine!
'Tis a fair world: if dark, indeed, with woe,
Yet having hope and hint of such a joy,
That a man, winning, well might turn aside,
Careless of Heaven...

                  O enough; I turn
From the sun's light, or haply I shall hope.
I have hoped enough; I would not hope again:
'Tis hope that is most cruel.

                    Tom, my friend,
You very sorry philosophic fool;
'Tis you, I think, that bid me be resign'd,
Trust, and be thankful.

                    Out on you! Resign'd?
I'm not resign'd, not patient, not school'd in
To take my starveling's portion and pretend
I'm grateful for it. I want all, all, all;
I've appetite for all. I want the best:
Love, beauty, sunlight, nameless joy of life.
There's too much patience in the world, I think.
We have grown base with crooking of the knee.
Mankind—say—God has bidden to a feast;
The board is spread, and groans with cates and drinks;
In troop the guests; each man with appetite
Keen-whetted with expectance.

                    In they troop,
Struggle for seats, jostle and push and seize.
What's this? what's this? There are not seats for all!
Some men must stand without the gates; and some
Must linger by the table, ill-supplied
With broken meats. One man gets meat for two,
The while another hungers. If I stand
Without the portals, seeing others eat
Where I had thought to satiate the pangs
Of mine own hunger; shall I then come forth
When all is done, and drink my Lord's good health
In my Lord's water? Shall I not rather turn

And curse him, curse him for a niggard host?
O, I have hungered, hungered, through the years,
Till appetite grows craving, then disease;
I am starved, wither'd, shrivelled.

                     Peace, O peace!
This rage is idle; what avails to curse
The nameless forces, the vast silences
That work in all things.

                 This time is the third,
I wrought before in heat, stung mad with pain,
Blind, scarcely understanding; now I know
What thing I do.

               There was a woman once;
Deep eyes she had, white hands, a subtle smile,
Soft speaking tones: she did not break my heart,
Yet haply had her heart been otherwise
Mine had not now been broken. Yet, who knows?
My life was jarring discord from the first:
Tho' here and there brief hints of melody,
Of melody unutterable, clove the air.
From this bleak world, into the heart of night,
The dim, deep bosom of the universe,
I cast myself. I only crave for rest;
Too heavy is the load. I fling it down.

We knocked and knocked; at last, burst in the door,
And found him as you know—the outstretched arms
Propping the hidden face. The sun had set,
And all the place was dim with lurking shade.
There was no written word to say farewell,
Or make more clear the deed.

                I search'd and search'd;
The room held little: just a row of books
Much scrawl'd and noted; sketches on the wall,
Done rough in charcoal; the old instrument
(A violin, no Stradivarius)
He played so ill on; in the table drawer
Large schemes of undone work. Poems half-writ;
Wild drafts of symphonies; big plans of fugues;
Some scraps of writing in a woman's hand:
No more—the scattered pages of a tale,
A sorry tale that no man cared to read.
Alas, my friend, I lov'd him well, tho' he
Held me a cold and stagnant-blooded fool,
Because I am content to watch, and wait
With a calm mind the issue of all things.
Certain it is my blood's no turbid stream;
Yet, for all that, haply I understood
More than he ever deem'd; nor held so light
The poet in him. Nay, I sometimes doubt
If they have not, indeed, the better part—

These poets, who get drunk with sun, and weep
Because the night or a woman's face is fair.
Meantime there is much talk about my friend.
The women say, of course, he died for love;
The men, for lack of gold, or cavilling
Of carping critics. I, Tom Leigh, his friend
I have no word at all to say of this.
Nay, I had deem'd him more philosopher;
For did he think by this one paltry deed
To cut the knot of circumstance, and snap
The chain which binds all being?

Medea

A Fragment in Drama Form, after Euripides

παντων δ'οσ εστ' εμψυχα και γνωμην εχει
γυναικεσ εσμεν αθλιωτατον φυτον.

PERSONS.

MEDEA.   ÆGEUS. } Citizens of Corinth.
JASON.   NIKIAS.

Scene: Before MEDEA's *House.*

[*Enter* MEDEA.]

MEDEA

To-day, to-day, I know not why it is,
I do bethink me of my Colchian home.
To-day, that I am lone and weary and sad,
I fain would call back days of pride and hope;
Of pride in strength, when strength was all unprov'd,
Of hope too high, too sweet, to be confined
In limits of conception.

          I am sad
Here in this gracious city, whose white walls
Gleam snow-like in the sunlight; whose fair shrines

Are filled with wondrous images of gods;
Upon whose harbour's bosom ride tall ships,
Black-masted, fraught with fragrant merchandise;
Whose straight-limbed people, in fair stuffs arrayed,
Do throng from morn till eve the sunny streets.
For what avail fair shrines and images?
What, cunning workmanship and purple robes?
Light of sweet sunlight, play and spray of waves?
When all around the air is charged and chill,
And all the place is drear and dark with hate?
Alas, alas, this people loves me not!
This strong, fair people, marble-cold and smooth
As modelled marble. I, an alien here,
That well can speak the language of their lips,
The language of their souls may never learn.
And in their hands, I, that did know myself
Ere now, a creature in whose veins ran blood
Redder, more rapid, than flows round most hearts,
Do seem a creature reft of life and soul.
If they would only teach the subtle trick
By which their hearts are melted into love,
I'd strive to learn it. I am very meek.
They think me proud, but I am very meek,
Ready to do their bidding. Hear me, friends!
Friends, I am very hungry, give me love!
'Tis all I ask! is it so hard to give?
You stand and front me with your hostile eyes;
You only give me hatred?

Yet I know
Ye are not all unloving. Oft I see
The men and women walking in the ways,
Hand within hand, and tender-bated breath,
On summer evenings when the sky is fair.
O men and women, are ye then so hard?
Will ye not give a little of your love
To me that am so hungry?

[*Enter* ÆGEUS *and* NIKIAS, *on the opposite side.*
MEDEA *steps back on the threshold and pauses.*]

Ha, that word!
'Tis Jason's name they bandy to and fro.
I know not why, whene'er his name is spoke,
Once name of joy and ever name of love,
I wax white and do tremble; sudden seized
With shadowy apprehension. May't forbode
No evil unto him I hold so dear;
And ever dearer with the waxing years:—
For this indeed is woman's chiefest curse,
That still her constant heart clings to its love
Through all time and all chances; while the man
Is caught with newness; coldly calculates,
And measures pain and pleasure, loss and gain;
And ever grows to look with the world's eye
Upon a woman, tho' his, body and soul.

[*She goes within. The two citizens come forward.*]

NIKIAS

I, in this thing, do hold our Jason wise;
Kreon is mighty; Glaukê very fair.

ÆGEUS

An 'twere for that—the Colchian's fair enough.

NIKIAS

I like not your swart skins and purple hair;
Your black, fierce eyes where the brows meet across.
By all the gods! when yonder Colchian
Fixes me with her strange and sudden gaze,
Each hair upon my body stands erect!
Zeus, 'tis a very tiger, and as mute!

ÆGEUS

'Tis certain that the woman's something strange.

NIKIAS

Gods, spare me your strange women, so say I.
Give me gold hair, lithe limbs and gracious smiles,
And spare the strangeness.

ÆGEUS

              I do marvel much
How she will bear the tidings.

NIKIAS

Lo, behold!
Here comes our Jason striding 'thwart the streets.
Gods! what a gracious presence!

ÆGEUS

I perceive
The Colchian on the threshold. By her looks,
Our idle talk has reached her listening ears.

[*Enter* JASON. MEDEA *reappears on the threshold.*]

NIKIAS

Let's draw aside and mark them; lo, they meet.

[*The two citizens withdraw, unperceived,
to a further corner of the stage.*]

MEDEA

'Tis false, 'tis false. O Jason, they speak false!

JASON

Your looks are wild, Medea; you bring shame
Upon this house, that stand with hair unbound
Beyond the threshold. Get you in the house.

MEDEA

But not till you have answered me this thing.

JASON

What is this thing that you would know of me?

MEDEA

O I have heard strange rumours—horrible!

JASON

Oft lies the horror of a tale in the ear
Of him that hears it. What is 't you have heard?

MEDEA

Almost, for fear, I dare not give it tongue.
But tell me this? Love, you have not forgot
The long years passed in this Corinthian home?
The great love I have borne you through the years?
Nor that far time when, in your mighty craft,
You came, a stranger, to the Colchian shore?
O strong you were; but not of such a strength
To have escaped the doom of horrid death,
Had not I, counting neither loss nor gain,
Shown you the way to triumph and renown.

JASON

And better had I then, a thousand times,
Have fought with my good sword and fall'n or stood

As the high Fates directed; than been caught
In the close meshes of the magic web
Wrought by your hand, dark-thoughted sorceress.

NIKIAS

Did you mark that? Jason speaks low and smooth;
Yet there is that within his level tones,
And in the icy drooping of his lids
(More than his words, tho' they are harsh enough),
Tells me he hates her.

ÆGEUS

Hush! Medea speaks.

MEDEA

O gods, gods; ye have cursed me in this gift!
Is it for this, for this that I have striven?
Have wrestled in the darkness? wept my tears?
Have fought with sweet desires and hopes and thoughts?
Have watched when men were sleeping? for long days
Have shunned the sunlight and the breaths of Heaven?
Is it for this, for this that I have prayed
Long prayers, poured out with blood and cries and tears?
Lo, I who strove for strength have grown more weak
Than is the weakest. I have poured the sap
Of all my being, my life's very life,
Before a thankless godhead; and am grown
No woman, but a monster. What avail

Charms, spells and potions, all my hard-won arts,
My mystic workings, seeing they cannot win
One little common spark of human love?
O gods, gods, ye have cursed me in this gift!
More should ye have withheld or more have giv'n;
Have fashioned me more weak or else more strong.
Behold me now, your work, a thing of fear—
From natural human fellowship cut off,
And yet a woman—sick and sore with pain;
Hungry for love and music of men's praise,
But walled about as with a mighty wall,
Far from men's reach and sight, alone, alone.

NIKIAS

Behold her, how she waves about her arms
And casts her eyes to Heaven.

ÆGEUS

                Ay, 'tis strange —
Not as our women do, yet scarce unmeet.

NIKIAS

Unmeet, unmeet? But Jason holds it so!
Mark you his white cheeks and his knitted brows,
What wrath and hate and scorn upon his face!

JASON

Hear me, Medea, if you still can hear

That seem so strangely lifted from yourself:
But I, that know you long, do know you well,
A thing of moods and passions; so I bear
Once more with your wild words and savage gests,
Ay, and for all your fury speak you fair.
You say you love me. Can I deem it so,
When what does most advantage me and mine
You shrink to hear of? For I make no doubt,
Fleet-footed rumour did anticipate
The tidings I was hastening to bear,
When you, wide-eyed, unveiled, unfilleted,
Rushed out upon me.

              Know then this once more:
That I have sworn to take as wedded wife
Glaukê, the daughter of our mighty king,
In this, in nowise hurting you and yours.
For you all fair provisions I have made,
So but you get beyond the city walls
Before the night comes on. Our little ones—
They too shall journey with you. I have said.
And had I found you in a mood more mild,
Less swayed by savage passion, I had told
How this thing, which mayhap seems a thing hard,
Is but a blessing, wrapped and cloaked about
In harsh disguisements. For tho' Kreon rule
To-day within the city; Kreon dead,
Who else shall rule there saving I alone,
The king's son loved of him and other men?

And in those days Medea's sons and mine
Shall stand at my right hand, grown great in power.
Medea, too, if she do but control
Her fiery spirit, may yet reign a queen
Above this land of Corinth. I have said.

NIKIAS

Well said.

ÆGEUS

But none the better that 'twas false.

NIKIAS

I'd sooner speak, for my part, fair than true.
Mark Jason there; how firm his lithe, straight limbs;
How high his gold-curled head, crisped like a girl's.
And yet for all his curled locks and smooth tones
Jason is very strong. I never knew
A man of such a strange and subtle strength.

ÆGEUS

The Colchian speaks no word; and her swart hands,
Which waved, a moment since, and beat the air
In mad entreaty, are together clasped
Before her white robe in an iron clasp.
And her wild eyes, which erst did seek the heav'ns,
And now her lord and now again the earth,
Are set on space and move not. The tall shape

Stands there erect and still. This calm, I think,
Is filled with strangest portent.

NIKIAS

                            O ye gods,
She is a pregnant horror as she stands.

ÆGEUS

She speaks; her voice sounds as a sound far off.

MEDEA

As you have said, O Jason, let it be.
I for my part am nothing loth to break
A compact never in fair justice framed,
Seeing how much one gave and one how much.
For you, you thought: This maid has served me well,
And yet may serve me. When I touch her palm
The blood is set a-tingle in my veins;
For these things I will make her body mine.
And I, I stood before you, clean and straight,
A woman some deemed fair and all deemed wise;
A woman, yet no simple thing nor slight,
By nature fashioned in no niggard mould;
And looked into your eyes with eyes that spake:
Lo, utterly, for ever, I am yours.
And since that you, this gift I lavish laid
Low at your feet, have lightly held and spurned—
I in my two arms, thus, shall gather it up

So that your feet may not encounter it
Which is not worthy for your feet to tread!
Yet pause a moment, Jason. Haply now
In some such wise as this your thoughts run on:
I loved this woman for a little space;
Alas, poor soul, she loved me but too well—
It is the way with women! Some, I think,
Did deem her fierce; gods! she was meek enough,
Content with what I gave; when I gave not
Nothing importunate.

                  Ah, Jason, pause.
You never knew Medea. You forget,
Because so long she bends the knee to you,
She was not born to serfdom.

                     I have knelt
Too long before you. I have stood too long
Suppliant before this people. You forget
A redder stream flows in my Colchian veins
Than the slow flood which courses round your hearts,
O cold Corinthians, with whom I long have dwelt
And never ere this day have known myself.
Nor have ye known me. Now behold me free,
Ungyved by any chains of this man wrought;
Nothing desiring at your hands nor his.
Free, freer than the air or wingèd birds;
Strong, stronger than the blast of wintry storms;
And lifted up into an awful realm

Where is nor love, nor pity, nor remorse,
Nor dread, but only purpose.
                              There shall be
A horror and a horror in this land;
Woe upon woe, red blood and biting flame;
Most horrid death and anguish worse than death;
Deeds that shall make the shores of Hades sound
With murmured terror; with an awful dread
Shall move the generations yet unborn;
A horror and a horror in the land.

JASON
Shrew, triple-linked with Hell, get you within.
Shame not my house! 'Tis your own harm you work.

[MEDEA *goes within.* JASON *moves off slowly.*
ÆGEUS *and* NIKIAS *go off conferring in whispers.*]

SCENE II

[*Time—After an interval; the evening of the same day.*
Scene—A street. A crowd of people running to and fro.]

NIKIAS

O horror, horror, have ye heard the tale?

ÆGEUS

Alas, a bloody rumour reached mine ears
Of awful purport: that the king lies dead—

NIKIAS

And by his side, his daughter; both caught up
In sudden toils of torment. With his grief
Jason is all distraught; behold her deed,
The swift and subtle tigress!

ÆGEUS

Woe! Alas! Woe for the state, woe for our Kreon slain,
For hapless Glaukê, for our Jason, woe!
But three times woe for her that did the deed—
Her womanhood sham'd; her children basely wrong'd.

NIKIAS

Hold back our pity till the tale be told,
For never was there horror like to this.
Ere now in Corinth, haply, you have heard

How she did use for her crime's instruments
The tender boys sprung from great Jason's loins;
Bidding them bear the garments wrought in Hell
As bridal gifts to grace the marriage morn
Of gold-hair'd Glaukê. Serpent! Sorceress!

ÆGEUS

Alas, consider; so the tigress springs
When that her cubs are menaced. 'Twas her love
That wrought the deed—evil, yet wrought for love.

NIKIAS

Spare me such love. I never yet could deem,
Ev'n ere the horror, that Medea held
The love of human mothers in her breast.
For I have seen her, when her children played
Their innocent, aimless sports about her knees,
Or held her gown across the market-place,
Move all unheeding with her swart brows knit
And fierce eyes fixed; not, as is mothers' wont,
Eager to note the winning infant ways,
A-strain to catch the babbling treble tones
Of soft lips clamouring for a kiss or smile.
And once I marked her ('twas a summer's morn)
Turn suddenly and, stooping, catch and strain
One tender infant to her breast. She held
Her lips to his and looked into his eyes,
Not gladly, as a mother with her child,

But stirred by some strange passion; then the boy
Cried out with terror, and Medea wept.

ÆGEUS
Your tale is strange.

NIKIAS
                    Stranger is yet to come.
How that the Colchian did send forth her sons,
Innocent doers of most deadly deed,
Has reached your knowledge. When the deed was done,
And the dead king lay stretched upon the floor
Clutching his daughter in a last embrace,
Arose great clamour in the palace halls;
Wailing and cries of terror; women's screams;
A rush of flying feet from hall to hall;
The clanging fall of brazen instruments
Upon the marble.
                    The two tender boys,
Half apprehending what thing had befallen,
Fled forth unmarked, and all affrighted reached
The house of Jason, where Medea stood
Erect upon the threshold. From afar
Sounded and surged the fiercely frighted roar
Of the roused city, and, like waves of the sea,
Grew nearer ev'ry beating of the pulse.
Forth from the inmost chambers fled the slaves,
Made fleet with sudden fear; the little ones

With arms outspread rushed to the Colchian,
And clung about her limbs and caught her robe,
Hiding their faces.

     And Medea stood
Calm as a carven image. As the sound
Of wrath and lamentation drew more near,
The pale lips seemed to smile. But when she saw
Her children clinging round her, she stretched forth
One strong, swart hand and put the twain away,
And gathered up the trailing of her robe.
I saw the deed, I, Nikias, with these eyes!
Then spake she (Zeus! grant that I may not hear
Such tones once more from human lips!). She spake:
"I will not have ye, for I love ye not!"
Then all her face grew alien. Those around
Stood still, not knowing what she planned.

       Then she
Forth from her gathered garment swiftly drew
A thing that gleamed and glinted; in the air
She held it poised an instant; then—O gods!
How shall I speak it?—on the marble floor
Was blood that streamed and spurted; blood that flow'd
From two slain, innocent babes!

ÆGEUS
   O woful day!

NIKIAS

Then brake a cry from all about: a wail
Of lamentation. But above the sound
A fierce long shriek, that froze the blood i' the veins,
Rang out and rose, cleaving the topmost cloud.

ÆGEUS

O evil deed! O essence of all evil
Stealing the shape of woman!

NIKIAS

After that
All is confusion; from all sides surged up
The people, cursing, weeping. 'Thwart the din
Each other moment the strained ear might catch
Medea's name, or Jason's, or the King's;
And women wailed out "Glaukê" through their tears.
Then sudden came a pause; the angry roar
Died down into a murmur; and the throng
Grew still, and rolled aside like a clov'n sea.
And Jason strode between them till he reached
His own home's threshold where the twain lay dead,
Long gazed he on their faces; then he turned
To the hush'd people; turned to them and spake:
(His face was whiter than the dead's, his eyes
Like to a creature's that has looked on Hell)
"Where is the woman?" Lo, and when they sought
Medea, no eye beheld her. And no man

Had looked upon her since that moment's space
When steel had flashed and blood foamed in the air.
Then Jason stood erect and spake again:
"Let no man seek this woman; blood enough
Has stained our city. Let the furies rend
Her guilty soul; nor we pollute our hands
With her accursèd body…"

ÆGEUS

       Cease, my friend;
It is enough. You judged this thing aright;
This woman was dark and evil in her soul;
Black to her fiend-heart's root; a festering plague
In our fair city's midst.

NIKIAS

       Spake I not true?

[*Night; outside the city.* MEDEA *leaning against a rock.*]

MEDEA

Here let me rest; beyond men's eyes, beyond
The city's hissing hate. Why am I here?
Why have I fled from death? There's sun on the earth,
And in the shades no sun;—thus much I know;
And sunlight's good.
       Wake I, or do I sleep?

I'm weary, weary; once I dream'd a dream
Of one that strove and wept and yearned for love
In a fair city. She was blind indeed.
They say the woman had a fiend at heart,
And afterwards—Hush, hush, I dream'd a dream.
How cold the air blows; how the night grows dark,
Wrapping me round in blackness. Darker too
Grows the deep night within. I cannot see;
I grope with weary hands; my hands are sore
With fruitless striving. I have fought with the Fates
And I am vanquished utterly. The Fates
Yield not to strife; nay, nor to many prayers.
Their ways are dark.
                        One climbs the tree and grasps
A handful of dead leaves; another walks,
Heedless, beneath the branches, and the fruit
Falls mellow at his feet.
                        This is the end:
I have dash'd my heart against a rock; the blood
Is drain'd and flows no more; and all my breast
Is emptied of its tears.
                        Thus go I forth
Into the deep, dense heart of the night—alone.

Sinfonia Eroica

To Sylvia

My Love, my Love, it was a day in June,
A mellow, drowsy, golden afternoon;
And all the eager people thronging came
To that great hall, drawn by the magic name
Of one, a high magician, who can raise
The spirits of the past and future days,
And draw the dreams from out the secret breast,
Giving them life and shape.
                        I, with the rest,
Sat there athirst, atremble for the sound;
And as my aimless glances wandered round,
Far off, across the hush'd, expectant throng,
I saw your face that fac'd mine.
                              Clear and strong
Rush'd forth the sound, a mighty mountain stream;
Across the clust'ring heads mine eyes did seem
By subtle forces drawn, your eyes to meet.
Then you, the melody, the summer heat,
Mingled in all my blood and made it wine.
Straight I forgot the world's great woe and mine;
My spirit's murky lead grew molten fire;
Despair itself was rapture.

Ever higher,
Stronger and clearer rose the mighty strain;
Then sudden fell; then all was still again,
And I sank back, quivering as one in pain.
Brief was the pause; then, 'mid a hush profound,
Slow on the waiting air swell'd forth a sound
So wondrous sweet that each man held his breath;
A measur'd, mystic melody of death.
Then back you lean'd your head, and I could note
The upward outline of your perfect throat;
And ever, as the music smote the air,
Mine eyes from far held fast your body fair.
And in that wondrous moment seem'd to fade
My life's great woe, and grow an empty shade
Which had not been, nor was not.
                                    And I knew
Not which was sound, and which, O Love, was you.

To Sylvia

"O love, lean thou thy cheek to mine,
And let the tears together flow"—
Such was the song you sang to me
Once, long ago.

Such was the song you sang; and yet
(O be not wroth!) I scarcely knew
What sounds flow'd forth; I only felt
That you were you.

I scarcely knew your hair was gold,
Nor of the heavens' own blue your eyes.
Sylvia and song, divinely mixt,
Made Paradise.

These things I scarcely knew; to-day,
When love is lost and hope is fled,
The song you sang so long ago
Rings in my head.

Clear comes each note and true; to-day,
As in a picture I behold
Your turn'd-up chin, and small, sweet head
Misty with gold.

I see how your dear eyes grew deep,
How your lithe body thrilled and swayed,
And how were whiter than the keys
        Your hands that played...

Ah, sweetest! cruel have you been,
And robbed my life of many things.
I will not chide; ere this I knew
        That Love had wings.

You've robbed my life of many things—
Of love and hope, of fame and pow'r.
So be it, sweet. You cannot steal
        One golden hour.

A Greek Girl

I may not weep, not weep, and he is dead.
A weary, weary weight of tears unshed
Through the long day in my sad heart I bear;
The horrid sun with all unpitying glare
Shines down into the dreary weaving-room,
Where clangs the ceaseless clatter of the loom,
And ceaselessly deft maiden-fingers weave
The fine-wrought web; and I from morn till eve
Work with the rest, and when folk speak to me
I smile hard smiles; while still continually
The silly stream of maiden speech flows on:—
And now at length they talk of him that's gone,
Lightly lamenting that he died so soon—
Ah me! ere yet his life's sun stood at noon.
Some praise his eyes, some deem his body fair,
And some mislike the colour of his hair!
Sweet life, sweet shape, sweet eyes, and sweetest hair,
What form, what hue, save Love's own, did ye wear?
I may not weep, not weep, for very shame.

He loved me not. One summer's eve he came
To these our halls, my father's honoured guest,
And seeing me, saw not. If his lips had prest
My lips, but once, in love; his eyes had sent

One love-glance into mine, I had been content,
And deemed it great joy for one little life;
Nor envied other maids the crown of wife:
The long sure years, the merry children-band—
Alas, alas, I never touched his hand!
And now my love is dead that loved not me.

Thrice-blest, thrice-crowned, of gods thrice-lovèd she—
That other, fairer maid, who tombward brings
Her gold, shorn locks and piled-up offerings
Of fragrant fruits, rich wines, and spices rare,
And cakes with honey sweet, with saffron fair;
And who, unchecked by any thought of shame,
May weep her tears, and call upon his name,
With burning bosom prest to the cold ground,
Knowing, indeed, that all her life is crown'd,
Thrice-crowned, thrice-honoured, with that love of his;—
No dearer crown on earth is there, I wis.

While yet the sweet life lived, more light to bear
Was my heart's hunger; when the morn was fair,
And I with other maidens in a line
Passed singing through the city to the shrine,
Oft in the streets or crowded market-place
I caught swift glimpses of the dear-known face;
Or marked a stalwart shoulder in the throng;
Or heard stray speeches as we passed along,
In tones more dear to me than any song.

These, hoarded up with care, and kept apart,
Did serve as meat and drink my hungry heart.

And now for ever has my sweet love gone;
And weary, empty days I must drag on,
Till all the days of all my life be sped,
By no thought cheered, by no hope comforted.
For if indeed we meet among the shades,
How shall he know me from the other maids?—
Me, that had died to save his body pain!

Alas, alas, such idle thoughts are vain!
O cruel, cruel sunlight, get thee gone!
O dear, dim shades of eve, come swiftly on!
That when quick lips, keen eyes, are closed in sleep,
Through the long night till dawn I then may weep.

Magdalen

All things I can endure, save one.
The bare, blank room where is no sun;
The parcelled hours; the pallet hard;
The dreary faces here within;
The outer women's cold regard;
The Pastor's iterated "sin"; —
These things could I endure, and count
No overstrain'd, unjust amount;
No undue payment for such bliss —
Yea, all things bear, save only this:
That you, who knew what thing would be,
Have wrought this evil unto me.
It is so strange to think on still —
That you, that you should do me ill!
Not as one ignorant or blind,
But seeing clearly in your mind
How this must be which now has been,
Nothing aghast at what was seen.
Now that the tale is told and done,
It is so strange to think upon.

You were so tender with me, too!
One summer's night a cold blast blew,
Closer about my throat you drew

The half-slipt shawl of dusky blue.
And once my hand, on a summer's morn,
I stretched to pluck a rose; a thorn
Struck through the flesh and made it bleed
(A little drop of blood indeed!)
Pale grew your cheek; you stoopt and bound
Your handkerchief about the wound;
Your voice came with a broken sound;
With the deep breath your breast was riven;
I wonder, did God laugh in Heaven?

How strange, that *you* should work my woe!
How strange! I wonder, do you know
How gladly, gladly I had died
(And life was very sweet that tide)
To save you from the least, light ill?
How gladly I had borne your pain.
With one great pulse we seem'd to thrill,—
Nay, but we thrill'd with pulses twain.

Even if one had told me this,
"A poison lurks within your kiss,
Gall that shall turn to night his day":
Thereon I straight had turned away—
Ay, tho' my heart had crack'd with pain—
And never kiss'd your lips again.

At night, or when the daylight nears,
I hear the other women weep;
My own heart's anguish lies too deep
For the soft rain and pain of tears.
I think my heart has turn'd to stone,
A dull, dead weight that hurts my breast;
Here, on my pallet-bed alone,
I keep apart from all the rest.
Wide-eyed I lie upon my bed,
I often cannot sleep all night;
The future and the past are dead,
There is no thought can bring delight.
All night I lie and think and think;
If my heart were not made of stone,
But flesh and blood, it needs must shrink
Before such thoughts. Was ever known
A woman with a heart of stone?

The doctor says that I shall die.
It may be so, yet what care I?
Endless reposing from the strife?
Death do I trust no more than life.
For one thing is like one arrayed,
And there is neither false nor true;
But in a hideous masquerade
All things dance on, the ages through.
And good is evil, evil good;
Nothing is known or understood

Save only Pain. I have no faith
In God or Devil, Life or Death.

The doctor says that I shall die.
You, that I knew in days gone by,
I fain would see your face once more,
Con well its features o'er and o'er;
And touch your hand and feel your kiss,
Look in your eyes and tell you this:
That all is done, that I am free;
That you, through all eternity,
Have neither part nor lot in me.

Christopher Found

I

At last; so this is you, my dear!
How should I guess to find you here?
So long, so long, I sought in vain
In many cities, many lands,
With straining eyes and groping hands;
The people marvelled at my pain.
They said: "But sure, the woman's mad;
What ails her, we should like to know,
That she should be so wan and sad,
And silent through the revels go?"
They clacked with such a sorry stir!
Was I to tell? were they to know
That I had lost you, Christopher?
Will you forgive me for one thing?
Whiles, when a stranger came my way,
My heart would beat and I would say:
"Here's Christopher!" — then lingering
With longer gaze, would turn away
Cold, sick at heart. My dear, I know
You will forgive me for this thing.
It is so very long ago
Since I have seen your face — till now;

Now that I see it—lip and brow,
Eyes, nostril, chin, alive and clear;
Last time was long ago; I know
This thing you will forgive me, dear.

II

There is no Heaven—This is the best;
O hold me closer to your breast;
Let your face lean upon my face,
That there no longer shall be space
Between our lips, between our eyes.
I feel your bosom's fall and rise.
O hold me near and yet more near;
Ah sweet; I wonder do you know
How lone and cold, how sad and drear,
Was I a little while ago;
Sick of the stress, the strife, the stir;
But I have found you, Christopher.

III

If only you had come before!
(This is the thing I most deplore)
A seemlier woman you had found,
More calm, by courtesies more bound,

Less quick to greet you, more subdued
Of appetite; of slower mood.
But ah! you come so late, so late!
This time of day I can't pretend
With slight, sweet things to satiate
The hunger-cravings. Nay, my friend,
I cannot blush and turn and tremble,
Wax loth as younger maidens do.
Ah, Christopher, with you, with you,
You would not wish me to dissemble?

IV

So long have all the days been meagre,
With empty platter, empty cup,
No meats nor sweets to do me pleasure,
That if I crave — is it over-eager,
The deepest draught, the fullest measure,
The beaker to the brim poured up?

V

Shelley, that sprite from the spheres above,
Says, and would make the matter clear,
That love divided is larger love; —
We'll leave those things to the bards, my dear.

For you never wrote a verse, you see;
And I—my verse is not fair nor new.
Till the world be dead, you shall love but me,
Till the stars have ceased, I shall love but you.

EPILOGUE

Thus ran the words; or rather, thus did run
Their purport. Idly seeking in the chest
(You see it yonder), I had found them there:
Some blotted sheets of paper in a case,
With a woman's name writ on it: "Adelaide."
Twice on the writing there was scored the date
Of ten years back; and where the words had end
Was left a space, a dash, a half-writ word,
As tho' the writer minded, presently
The matter to pursue.

      I questioned her,
That worthy, worthy soul, my châtelaine,
Who, nothing loth, made answer.

         There had been
Another lodger ere I had the rooms,
Three months gone by—a woman.

         "Young, sir? No.
Must have seen forty if she'd seen a day!
A lonesome woman; hadn't many friends;
Wrote books, I think, and things for newspapers.

Short in her temper—eyes would flash and flame
At times, till I was frightened. Paid her rent
Most regular, like a lady.

                Ten years back,
They say (at least Ann Brown says), ten years back
The lady had a lover. Even then
She must have been no chicken.

                     Three months since
She died. Well, well, the Lord is kind and just.
I did my best to tend her, yet indeed
It's bad for trade to have a lodger die.
Her brother came, a week before she died:
Buried her, took her things, threw in the fire
The littered heaps of paper.

                  Yes, the sheets,
They must have been forgotten in the chest;—
I never knew her name was Adelaide."

A Dirge

"Mein Herz, mein Herz ist traurig,
Doch lustig leuchtet der Mai"

There's May amid the meadows,
    There's May amid the trees;
Her May-time note the cuckoo
    Sends forth upon the breeze.

Above the rippling river
    May swallows skim and dart;
November and December
    Keep watch within my heart.

The spring breathes in the breezes,
    The woods with wood-notes ring,
And all the budding hedgerows
    Are fragrant of the spring.

In secret, silent places
    The live green things upstart;
Ice-bound, ice-crown'd dwells winter
    For ever in my heart.

Upon the bridge I linger,
    Near where the lime-trees grow;
Above, swart birds are circling,
    Beneath, the stream runs slow.

A stripling and a maiden
    Come wand'ring up the way;
His eyes are glad with springtime,
    Her face is fair with May.

Of warmth and sun and sweetness
    All nature takes a part;
The ice of all the ages
    Weighs down upon my heart.

A June-Tide Echo

After a Richter Concert

In the long, sad time, when the sky was grey,
    And the keen blast blew through the city drear,
When delight had fled from the night and the day,
    My chill heart whispered, "June will be here!

June with its roses a-sway in the sun,
    Its glory of green on mead and tree."
Lo, now the sweet June-tide is nearly done,
    June-tide, and never a joy for me!

Is it so much of the gods that I pray?
    Sure craved man never so slight a boon!
To be glad and glad in my heart one day—
    One perfect day of the perfect June.

Sweet sounds to-night rose up, wave upon wave;
    Sweet dreams were afloat in the balmy air.
This is the boon of the gods that I crave—
    To be glad, as the music and night were fair.

For once, for one fleeting hour, to hold
    The fair shape the music that rose and fell

Revealed and concealed like a veiling fold;
    To catch for an instant the sweet June spell.

For once, for one hour, to catch and keep
    The sweet June secret that mocks my heart;
Now lurking calm, like a thing asleep,
    Now hither and thither with start and dart.

Then the sick, slow grief of the weary years,
    The slow, sick grief and the sudden pain;
The long days of labour, the nights of tears—
    No more these things would I hold in vain.

I would hold my life as a thing of worth;
    Pour praise to the gods for a precious thing.
Lo, June in her fairness is on earth,
    And never a joy does the niggard bring.

To Lallie

Outside the British Museum

Up those Museum steps you came,
And straightway all my blood was flame,
       O Lallie, Lallie!

The world (I had been feeling low)
In one short moment's space did grow
       A happy valley.

There was a friend, my friend, with you;
A meagre dame, in peacock blue
       Apparelled quaintly;

This poet-heart went pit-a-pat;
I bowed and smiled and raised my hat;
       You nodded—faintly.

My heart was full as full could be;
You had not got a word for me,
       Not one short greeting;

That nonchalant small nod you gave
(The tyrant's motion to the slave)
        Sole mark'd our meeting.

Is it so long? Do you forget
That first and last time that we met?
        The time was summer;

The trees were green; the sky was blue;
Our host presented me to you—
        A tardy comer.

You look'd demure, but when you spoke
You made a little, funny joke,
        Yet half pathetic.

Your gown was grey, I recollect,
I think you patronized the sect
        They call "æsthetic."

I brought you strawberries and cream,
I plied you long about a stream
        With duckweed laden;

We solemnly discussed the—heat.
I found you shy and very sweet,
        A rosebud maiden.

Ah me, to-day! You passed inside
To where the marble gods abide:
          Hermes, Apollo,

Sweet Aphrodite, Pan; and where,
For aye reclined, a headless fair
          Beats all fairs hollow.

And I, I went upon my way,
Well—rather sadder, let us say;
          The world looked flatter.

I had been sad enough before,
A little less, a little more,
          What does it matter?

In a Minor Key

An Echo from a Larger Lyre

That was love that I had before,
    Years ago, when my heart was young;
Ev'ry smile was a gem you wore,
    Ev'ry word was a sweet song sung.

You came — all my pulses burn'd and beat.
    (O sweet wild throbs of an early day!)
You went — with the last dear sound of your feet
    The light wax'd dim and the place grew grey.

And I us'd to pace with a stealthy tread
    By a certain house which is under a hill;
A cottage stands near, wall'd white, roof'd red —
    Tall trees grow thick — I can see it still!

How I us'd to watch with a hope that was fear
    For the least swift glimpse of your gown's dear fold!
(You wore blue gowns in those days, my dear —
    One light for summer, one dark for cold.)

Tears and verses I shed for you in show'rs;
    I would have staked my soul for a kiss;

Tribute daily I brought you of flow'rs,
    Rose, lily, your favourite eucharis.

There came a day we were doomed to part;
    There's a queer, small gate at the foot of a slope:
We parted there—and I thought my heart
    Had parted for ever from love and hope.

    *   *   *   *   *

Is it love that I have to-day?
    Love, that bloom'd early, has it bloom'd late
For me, that, clothed in my spirit's grey,
    Sit in the stillness and stare at Fate?

Song nor sonnet for you I've penned,
    Nor passionate paced by your home's wide wall
I have brought you never a flow'r, my friend,
    Never a tear for your sake let fall.

And yet—and yet—ah, who understands?
    We men and women are complex things!
A hundred tunes Fate's inexorable hands
    May play on the sensitive soul-strings.

Webs of strange patterns we weave (each owns)
    From colour and sound; and like unto these,
Soul has its tones and its semitones,
    Mind has its major and minor keys.

Your face (men pass it without a word)
    It haunts my dreams like an odd, sweet strain;
When your name is spoken my soul is stirr'd
    In its deepest depths with a dull, dim pain.

I paced, in the damp grey mist, last night
    In the streets (an hour) to see you pass:
Yet I do not think that I love you — quite;
    What's felt so finely 'twere coarse to class.

And yet — and yet — I scarce can tell why
    (As I said, we are riddles and hard to read),
If the world went ill with you, and I
    Could help with a hidden hand your need;

But, ere I could reach you where you lay,
    Must strength and substance and honour spend;
Journey long journeys by night and day —
    Somehow, I think I should come, my friend!

Last Words

"Dead! All's done with!"
R. BROWNING

These blossoms that I bring;
This song that here I sing;
These tears that now I shed;
I give unto the dead.

There is no more to be done,
Nothing, beneath the sun,
All the long ages through,
Nothing—by me for you.

The tale is told to the end;
This, ev'n, I may not know—
If we were friend and friend,
If we were foe and foe.

All's done with utterly,
All's done with. Death to me
Was ever Death indeed;
To me no kindly creed

Consolatory was given.
You were of earth, not Heaven...
This dreary day, things seem
Vain shadows in a dream,

Or some strange, pictured show;
And mine own tears that flow,
My hidden tears that fall,
The vainest of them all.

Philosophy in the Ballroom[1]

Ere all the world had grown so drear,
When I was young and you were here,
'Mid summer roses in summer weather,
What pleasant times we've had together!

We were not Phyllis, simple-sweet,
And Corydon; we did not meet
By brook or meadow, but among
A Philistine and flippant throng

Which much we scorned; (less rigorous
It had no scorn at all for us!)
How many an eve of sweet July,
Heedless of Mrs. Grundy's eye,

We've scaled the stairway's topmost height,
And sat there talking half the night;
And, gazing on the crowd below,
Thanked Fate and Heaven that made us so;—

1. First published in *London Society* 48. Reprinted in *A London Plane-Tree and other Verse* as "Philosophy".

To hold the pure delights of brain
Above light loves and sweet champagne.
For, you and I, we did eschew
The egoistic "I" and "you";

And all our observations ran
On Art and Letters, Life and Man.
Proudly we sat, we two, on high,
Throned in our Objectivity;

Scarce friends, not lovers (each avers),
But sexless, safe Philosophers.

*　　　　*　　　　*　　　　*

Dear Friend, you must not deem me light
If, as I lie and muse to-night,
I give a smile and not a sigh
To thoughts of our Philosophy.

Captivity

The lion remembers the forest,
    The lion in chains;
To the bird that is captive a vision
    Of woodland remains.

One strains with his strength at the fetter,
    In impotent rage;
One flutters in flights of a moment,
    And beats at the cage.

If the lion were loosed from the fetter,
    To wander again;
He would seek the wide silence and shadow
    Of his jungle in vain.

He would rage in his fury, destroying;
    Let him rage, let him roam!
Shall he traverse the pitiless mountain,
    Or swim through the foam?

If they opened the cage and the casement,
    And the bird flew away;
He would come back at evening, heartbroken,
    A captive for aye.

Would come if his kindred had spared him,
 Free birds from afar—
There was wrought what is stronger than iron
 In fetter and bar.

I cannot remember my country,
 The land whence I came;
Whence they brought me and chained me and made me
 Nor wild thing nor tame.

This only I know of my country,
 This only repeat:—
It was free as the forest, and sweeter
 Than woodland retreat.

When the chain shall at last be broken,
 The window set wide;
And I step in the largeness and freedom
 Of sunlight outside;

Shall I wander in vain for my country?
 Shall I seek and not find?
Shall I cry for the bars that encage me,
 The fetters that bind?

Lohengrin

Back to the mystic shore beyond the main
The mystic craft has sped, and left no trace.
    Ah, nevermore may she behold his face,
Nor touch his hand, nor hear his voice again!
With hidden front she crouches; all in vain
    The proffered balm. A vessel nears the place;
They bring her young, lost brother; see her strain
    The new-found nursling in a close embrace.

God, we have lost Thee with much questioning.
In vain we seek Thy trace by sea and land,
And in Thine empty fanes where no men sing.
    What shall we do through all the weary days?
    Thus wail we and lament. Our eyes we raise,
And, lo, our Brother with an outstretched hand!

To E.

The mountains in fantastic lines
Sweep, blue-white, to the sky, which shines
Blue as blue gems; athwart the pines
   The lake gleams blue.

We three were here, three years gone by;
Our Poet, with fine-frenzied eye,
You, stepped in learned lore, and I,
   A poet too.

Our Poet brought us books and flowers,
He read us *Faust*; he talked for hours
Philosophy (sad Schopenhauer's),
   Beneath the trees:

And do you mind that sunny day,
When he, as on the sward he lay,
Told of Lassalle who bore away
   The false Louise?

Thrice-favoured bard! to him alone
That green and snug retreat was shown,
Where to the vulgar herd unknown,
   Our pens we plied.

(For, in those distant days, it seems,
We cherished sundry idle dreams,
And with our flowing foolscap reams
      The Fates defied.)

And after, when the day was gone,
And the hushed, silver night came on,
He showed us where the glow-worm shone;—
      We stooped to see.

There, too, by yonder moon we swore
Platonic friendship o'er and o'er;
No folk, we deemed, had been before
      So wise and free.

*   *   *   *

And do I sigh or smile to-day?
Dead love or dead ambition, say,
Which mourn we most? Not much we weigh
      Platonic friends.

On you the sun is shining free;
Our Poet sleeps in Italy,
Beneath an alien sod; on me
      The cloud descends.

A Game of Lawn Tennis

What wonder that I should be dreaming
    Out here in the garden to-day?
The light through the leaves is streaming,—
      Paulina cries, "Play!"

The birds to each other are calling,
    The freshly-cut grasses smell sweet;
To Teddy's dismay, comes falling
      The ball at my feet.

"Your stroke should be over, not under!"
    "But that's such a difficult way!"
The place is a springtide wonder
      Of lilac and may;

Of lilac, and may, and laburnum,
    Of blossom,—*We'er losing the set!*
"Those volleys of Jenny's,—return them;
      "Stand close to the net! "

*   *   *   *

You are so fond of the Maytime,
    My friend, far away;
Small wonder that I should be dreaming
    Of you in the garden to-day.

Alma Mater

A haunted town thou art to me.
ANDREW LANG

To-day in Florence all the air
Is soft with spring, with sunlight fair;
In the tall street gay folks are met;
Duomo and Tower gleam overhead,
Like jewels in the city set,
Fair-hued and many-faceted.
Against the old grey stones are piled
February violets, pale and sweet,
Whose scent of earth in woodland wild
Is wafted up and down the street.
The city's heart is glad; my own
Sits lightly on its bosom's throne.

* * * *

Why is it that I see to-day,
Imaged as clear as in a dream,
A little city far away,
A churlish sky, a sluggish stream,
Tall clust'ring trees and gardens fair,
Dark birds that circle in the air,

Grey towers and fanes; on either hand,
Stretches of wind-swept meadow-land?

*   *   *   *

Oh, who can sound the human breast?
And this strange truth must be confessed;
That city do I love the best
Wherein my heart was heaviest!

The Two Terrors

Two terrors fright my soul by night and day:
The first is Life, and with her come the years;
A weary, winding train of maidens they,
With forward-fronting eyes, too sad for tears;
Upon whose kindred faces, blank and grey,
The shadow of a kindred woe appears.
Death is the second terror; who shall say
What form beneath the shrouding mantle nears?

Which way she turn, my soul finds no relief,
My smitten soul may not be comforted;
Alternately she swings from grief to grief,
And, poised between them, sways from dread to dread.
For there she dreads because she knows; and here,
Because she knows not, inly faints with fear.

London in July

What ails my senses thus to cheat?
    What is it ails the place,
That all the people in the street
    Should wear one woman's face?

The London trees are dusty-brown
    Beneath the summer sky;
My love, she dwells in London town,
    Nor leaves it in July.

O various and intricate maze,
    Wide waste of square and street;
Where, missing through unnumbered days,
    We twain at last may meet!

And who cries out on crowd and mart?
    Who prates of stream and sea?
The summer in the city's heart—
    That is enough for me.

Rondel

Dedicated to Mrs. Fenwick-Miller

To change my name was once my heart's desire!
In other days (I own it without shame)
I was a simple maid, who did aspire
        To change of name.

My dreams were undisturbed by thoughts of fame;
I was content to listen and admire
While Edwin told me of his hopes and aim.

Of such unworthy weakness now I tire;
I grow to recognize my sex's claim:
Married or single, I do *not* require
        To change my name.

Between the Showers[1]

Between the showers I went my way,
    The glistening street was bright with flowers;
It seemed that March had turned to May
        Between the showers.

Above the shining roofs and towers
    The blue broke forth athwart the grey;
Birds carolled in their leafless bowers.

Hither and tither, swift and gay,
    The people chased the changeful hours;
And you, you passed and smiled that day,
        Between the showers.

1. First published as "Roundel" in *Star*, February 29, 1888; published under the present title in *A London Plane-Tree*.

Straw in the Street

Straw in the street where I pass to-day
Dulls the sound of the wheels and feet.
'Tis for a failing life they lay
        Straw in the street.

Here, where the pulses of London beat,
Someone strives with the Presence grey;
Ah, is it victory or defeat?

The hurrying people go their way,
Pause and jostle and pass and greet;
For life, for death, are they treading, say,
        Straw in the street?

Ballade of an Omnibus

To see my love suffices me.
BALLADES IN BLUE CHINA

Some men to carriages aspire;
On some the costly hansoms wait;
Some seek a fly, on job or hire;
Some mount the trotting steed, elate.
I envy not the rich and great,
A wandering minstrel, poor and free,
I am contented with my fate—
An omnibus suffices me.

In winter days of rain and mire
I find within a corner strait;
The 'busmen know me and my lyre
From Brompton to the Bull-and-Gate.
When summer comes, I mount in state
The topmost summit, whence I see
Crœsus look up, compassionate—
An omnibus suffices me.

I mark, untroubled by desire,
Lucullus' phaeton and its freight.
The scene whereof I cannot tire,
The human tale of love and hate,
The city pageant, early and late
Unfolds itself, rolls by, to be
A pleasure deep and delicate.
An omnibus suffices me.

Princess, your splendour you require,
I, my simplicity; agree
Neither to rate lower nor higher.
An omnibus suffices me.

A London Plane-Tree

Green is the plane-tree in the square,
    The other trees are brown;
They droop and pine for country air;
    The plane-tree loves the town.

Here from my garret-pane, I mark
    The plane-tree bud and blow,
Shed her recuperative bark,
    And spread her shade below.

Among her branches, in and out,
    The city breezes play;
The dun fog wraps her round about;
    Above, the smoke curls grey.

Others the country take for choice,
    And hold the town in scorn;
But she has listened to the voice
    On city breezes borne.

Ballade of a Special Edition

He comes; I hear him up the street—
     Bird of ill omen, flapping wide
The pinion of a printed sheet,
     His hoarse note scares the eventide.
Of slaughter, theft, and suicide
     He is the herald and the friend;
Now he vociferates with pride—
     A double murder in Mile End!

A hanging to his soul is sweet;
     His gloating fancy's fain to bide
Where human-freighted vessels meet,
     And misdirected trains collide.
With Shocking Accidents supplied,
     He tramps the town from end to end.
How often have we heard it cried—
     A double murder in Mile End.

War loves he; victory or defeat,
     So there be loss on either side.
His tale of horrors incomplete,
     Imagination's aid is tried.
Since no distinguished man has died,
     And since the Fates, relenting, send

No great catastrophe, he's spied
    This double murder in Mile End.

Fiend, get thee gone! no more repeat
    Those sounds which do mine ears offend.
It is apocryphal, you cheat,
    Your double murder in Mile End.

The First Extra

A Waltz Song

O sway, and swing, and sway,
    And swing, and sway, and swing!
Ah me, what bliss like unto this,
    Can days and daylight bring?

A rose beneath your feet
    Has fallen from my head;
Its odour rises sweet,
    All crushed it lies, and dead.

O Love is like a rose,
    Fair-hued, of fragrant breath;
A tender flow'r that lives an hour,
    And is most sweet in death.

O swing, and sway, and swing,
    And rise, and sink, and fall!
There is no bliss like unto this,
    This is the best of all.

The Village Garden

To E. M. S.

Here, where your garden fenced about and still is,
 Here, where the unmoved summer air is sweet
With mixed delight of lavender and lilies,
 Dreaming I linger in the noontide heat.

Of many summers are the trees recorders,
 The turf a carpet many summers wove;
Old-fashioned blossoms cluster in the borders,
 Love-in-a-mist and crimson-hearted clove.

All breathes of peace and sunshine in the present,
 All tells of bygone peace and bygone sun,
Of fruitful years accomplished, budding, crescent,
 Of gentle seasons passing one by one.

Fain would I bide, but ever in the distance
 A ceaseless voice is sounding clear and low;—
The city calls me with her old persistence,
 The city calls me—I arise and go.

Of gentler souls this fragrant peace is guerdon;
    For me, the roar and hurry of the town,
Wherein more lightly seems to press the burden
    Of individual life that weighs me down.

I leave your garden to the happier comers
    For whom its silent sweets are anodyne.
Shall I return? Who knows, in other summers
    The peace my spirit longs for may be mine?

Translation from Heine[1]

They have told thee a-many stories,
    And much complaint have made;
And yet my heart's true anguish
    That never have they said.

They shook their heads protesting,
    They made a great to-do;
They called me a wicked fellow,
    And thou believdst it true.

And yet the worst of all things,
    Of that they were not aware,
The darkest and the saddest,
    That in my heart I bear.

1. From *Jewish Portraits*, edited by Katie Magnus, 1888.

Translations from Jehudah Halevi[1]

God grant that I may rise again,
Nor perish by Thine anger slain.
This draught that I myself combine,
What is it? Only Thou dost know
If well or ill, if swift or slow,
Its parts shall work upon my pain.
Ay, of these things, alone is Thine
The knowledge. All my faith I place,
Not in my craft, but in Thy grace.

*   *   *   *

Lo! my light has pierced to the dark abyss,
I have brought forth gems from the gloomy mine;
Now the fools would see them! I ask you this:
Shall I fling my pearls down before the swine?
From the gathered cloud shall the raindrops flow
To the barren land where no fruit can grow?

*   *   *   *

1. Jehudah Halevi (c. 1075–1141) was a Spanish-Jewish poet, philosopher, and physician. Levy made these translations of his Hebrew poetry from the German translations of Abraham Geiger.

So we must be divided; sweetest, stay,
     Once more, mine eyes would seek thy glance's light.
At night I shall recall thee: Thou, I pray,
     Be mindful of the days of our delight.
Come to me in my dreams, I ask of thee,
And even in my dreams be gentle unto me.

If thou shouldst send me greeting in the grave,
     The cold breath of the grave itself were sweet;
Oh, take my life, my life, 'tis all I have,
     If it should make thee live, I do entreat.
I think that I shall hear when I am dead,
The rustle of thy gown, thy footsteps overhead.

    *   *   *   *

A dove of rarest worth
And sweet exceedingly;
Alas, why does she turn
And fly so far from me?
In my fond heart a tent,
Should aye preparèd be.
My poor heart she has caught
With magic spells and wiles.
I do not sigh for gold,
But for her mouth that smiles;
Her hue it is so bright,
She half makes blind my sight

The day at last is here
Fill'd full of love's sweet fire;
The twain shall soon be one,
Shall stay their fond desire.
Ah! would my tribe could chance
On such deliverance.

*   *   *   *

Oh! city of the world, most chastely fair;
In the far west, behold I sigh for thee.
And in my yearning love I do bethink me,
Of bygone ages; of thy ruined fane,
Thy vanished splendour of a vanished day.
Oh! had I eagle's wings I'd fly to thee,
And with my falling tears make moist thine earth.
I long for thee; what though indeed thy kings
Have passed for ever; though where once up-rose
Sweet balsam-trees the serpent makes his nest.
Oh! that I might embrace thy dust, the sod
Were sweet as honey to my fond desire.

The Old House

In through the porch and up the silent stair;
    Little is changed, I know so well the ways;—
Here, the dead came to meet me; it was there
    The dream was dreamed in unforgotten days .

But who is this that hurries on before,
    A flitting shade the brooding shades among?—
She turned,—I saw her face,—O God! it wore
    The face I used to wear when I was young!

I thought my spirit and my heart were tamed
    To deadness; dead the pangs that agonise.
The old grief springs to choke me. —I am shamed
    Before that little ghost with eager eyes.

O turn away, let her not see, not know!
    How should she bear it, how should understand?
O hasten down the stairway, haste and go,
    And leave her dreaming in the silent land.

The Birch-Tree at Loschwitz

At Loschwitz above the city
    The air is sunny and chill;
The birch-trees and the pine-trees
    Grow thick upon the hill.

Lone and tall, with silver stem,
    A birch-tree stands apart;
The passionate wind of spring-time
    Stirs in its leafy heart.

I lean against the birch-tree,
    My arms around it twine;
It pulses, and leaps, and quivers,
    Like a human heart to mine.

One moment I stand, then sudden
    Let loose mine arms that cling:
O God! the lonely hillside,
    The passionate wind of spring!

A Wall Flower

I lounge in the doorway and languish in vain
While Tom, Dick and Harry are dancing with Jane.

My spirit rises to the music's beat;
There is a leaden fiend lurks in my feet!
To move unto your motion, Love, were sweet.

Somewhere, I think, some other where, not here,
In other ages, on another sphere,
I danced with you, and you with me, my dear.

In perfect motion did our bodies sway,
To perfect music that was heard alway;
Woe's me, that am so dull of foot to-day!

To move unto your motion, Love, were sweet;
My spirit rises to the music's beat—
But, ah, the leaden demon in my feet!

A March Day in London

The east wind blows in the street to-day;
The sky is blue, yet the town looks grey.
'Tis the wind of ice, the wind of fire,
Of cold despair and of hot desire,
Which chills the flesh to aches and pains,
And sends a fever through all the veins.

From end to end, with aimless feet,
All day long have I paced the street.
My limbs are weary, but in my breast
Stirs the goad of a mad unrest.
I would give anything to stay
The little wheel that turns in my brain;
The little wheel that turns all day,
That turns all night with might and main.

What is the thing I fear, and why?
Nay, but the world is all awry—
The wind's in the east, the sun's in the sky.

The gas-lamps gleam in a golden line;
The ruby lights of the hansoms shine,
Glance, and flicker like fire-flies bright;
The wind has fallen with the night,

And once again the town seems fair
Thwart the mist that hangs i' the air.

And o'er, at last, my spirit steals
A weary peace; peace that conceals
Within its inner depths the grain
Of hopes that yet shall flower again.

Out of Town

Out of town the sky was bright and blue,
　　Never fog-cloud, lowering, thick, was seen to frown;
Nature dons a garb of gayer hue,
　　　　Out of town.

Spotless lay the snow on field and down,
　　Pure and keen the air above it blew;
All wore peace and beauty for a crown.

London sky, marred by smoke, veiled from view,
　　London snow, trodden thin, dingy brown,
Whence that strange unrest at thoughts of you
　　　　Out of town?

The Piano-Organ

My student-lamp is lighted,
    The books and papers are spread;
A sound comes floating upwards,
    Chasing the thoughts from my head.

I open the garret window,
    Let the music in and the moon;
See the woman grin for coppers,
    While the man grinds out the tune.

Grind me a dirge or a requiem,
    Or a funeral-march sad and slow,
But not, O not, that waltz tune
    I heard so long ago.

I stand upright by the window,
    The moonlight streams in wan:—
O God! with its changeless rise and fall
    The tune twirls on and on.

London Poets

In Memoriam

They trod the streets and squares where now I tread,
With weary hearts, a little while ago;
When, thin and grey, the melancholy snow
Clung to the leafless branches overhead;
Or when the smoke-veiled sky grew stormy-red
In autumn; with a re-arisen woe
Wrestled, what time the passionate spring winds blow;
And paced scorched stones in summer:—they are dead.

The sorrow of their souls to them did seem
As real as mine to me, as permanent.
To-day, it is the shadow of a dream,
The half-forgotten breath of breezes spent.
So shall another soothe his woe supreme—
"No more he comes, who this way came and went."

New Love, New Life

I

She, who so long has lain
    Stone-stiff with folded wings,
Within my heart again
    The brown bird wakes and sings.

Brown nightingale, whose strain
    Is heard by day, by night,
She sings of joy and pain,
    Of sorrow and delight.

II

'Tis true,—in other days
    Have I unbarred the door;
He knows the walks and ways—
    Love has been here before.

Love blest and love accurst
    Was here in days long past;
This time is not the first,
    But this time is the last.

Impotens

If I were a woman of old,
　　What prayers I would pray for you, dear;
My pitiful tribute behold—
　　Not a prayer, but a tear.

The pitiless order of things,
　　Whose laws we may change not nor break,
Alone I could face it—it wrings
　　My heart for your sake.

Youth and Love

What does youth know of love?
　　Little enough, I trow!
He plucks the myrtle for his brow,
　　For his forehead the rose.
　　Nay, but of love
It is not youth who knows.

The Dream

Believe me, this was true last night,
Tho' it is false to-day.
A.M.F. ROBINSON.

A fair dream to my chamber flew:
Such a crowd of folk that stirred,
Jested, fluttered; only you,
You alone of all that band,
Calm and silent, spake no word.
Only once you neared my place,
And your hand one moment's space
Sought the fingers of my hand;
Your eyes flashed to mine; I knew
All was well between us two.

*   *   *   *

On from dream to dream I past,
But the first sweet vision cast
Mystic radiance o'er the last.

*   *   *   *

When I woke the pale night lay
Still, expectant of the day;
All about the chamber hung
Tender shade of twilight gloom;
The fair dream hovered round me, clung
To my thought like faint perfume:—
Like sweet odours, such as cling
To the void flask, which erst encloses
Attar of rose; or the pale string
Of amber which has lain with roses.

On the Threshold

O God, my dream! I dreamed that you were dead;
Your mother hung above the couch and wept
Whereon you lay all white, and garlanded
With blooms of waxen whiteness. I had crept
Up to your chamber-door, which stood ajar,
And in the doorway watched you from afar,
Nor dared advance to kiss your lips and brow.
I had no part nor lot in you, as now;
Death had not broken between us the old bar;
Nor torn from out my heart the old, cold sense
Of your misprision and my impotence.

In the Night

Cruel? I think there never was a cheating
    More cruel, thro' all the weary days than this!
This is no dream, my heart kept on repeating,
    But sober certainty of waking bliss.

Dreams? O, I know their faces—goodly seeming,
    Vaporous, whirled on many-coloured wings;
I have had dreams before, this is no dreaming,
    But daylight gladness that the daylight brings.

What ails my love; what ails her? She is paling;
    Faint grows her face, and slowly seems to fade!
I cannot clasp her—stretch out unavailing
    My arms across the silence and the shade.

Borderland

Am I waking, am I sleeping?
As the first faint dawn comes creeping
Thro' the pane, I am aware
Of an unseen presence hovering,
Round, above, in the dusky air:
A downy bird, with an odorous wing,
That fans my forehead, and sheds perfume,
As sweet as love, as soft as death,
Drowsy-slow through the summer-gloom.
My heart in some dream-rapture saith,
It is she. Half in a swoon,
I spread my arms in slow delight.—
O prolong, prolong the night,
For the nights are short in June!

At Dawn

In the night I dreamed of you;
    All the place was filled
With your presence; in my heart
    The strife was stilled.

All night I have dreamed of you;
    Now the morn is grey.—
How shall I arise and face
    The empty day?

June

Last June I saw your face three times;
    Three times I touched your hand;
Now, as before, May month is o'er,
    And June is in the land.

O many Junes shall come and go,
    Flow'r-footed o'er the mead;
O many Junes for me, to whom
    Is length of days decreed.

There shall be sunlight, scent of rose;
    Warm mist of summer rain;
Only this change—I shall not look
    Upon your face again.

A Reminiscence

It is so long gone by, and yet
    How clearly now I see it all!
The glimmer of your cigarette,
    The little chamber, narrow and tall.

Perseus; your picture in its frame;
    (How near they seem and yet how far!)
The blaze of kindled logs; the flame
    Of tulips in a mighty jar.

Florence and spring-time: surely each
    Glad things unto the spirit saith.
Why did you lead me in your speech
    To these dark mysteries of death?

The Sequel to "A Reminiscence"

Not in the street and not in the square,
  The street and square where you went and came;
With shuttered casement your house stands bare,
  Men hush their voice when they speak your name.

I, too, can play at the vain pretence,
  Can feign you dead; while a voice sounds clear
In the inmost depths of my heart: Go hence,
  Go, find your friend who is far from here.

Not here, but somewhere where I can reach!
  Can a man with motion, hearing and sight,
And a thought that answered my thought and speech,
  Be utterly lost and vanished quite?

Whose hand was warm in my hand last week? . . .
  My heart beat fast as I neared the gate —
Was it this I had come to seek,
  "A stone that stared with your name and date";

A hideous, turfless, fresh-made mound;
   A silence more cold than the wind that blew?
What had I lost, and what had I found?
   My flowers that mocked me fell to the ground—
Then, and then only, my spirit knew.

In the Mile End Road

How like her! But 'tis she herself,
    Comes up the crowded street,
How little did I think, the morn,
    My only love to meet!

Whose else that motion and that mien?
    Whose else that airy tread?
For one strange moment I forgot
    My only love was dead.

Contradictions

Now, even, I cannot think it true,
My friend, that there is no more you.
Almost as soon were no more I,
Which were, of course, absurdity!
Your place is bare, you are not seen,
Your grave, I'm told, is growing green;
And both for you and me, you know,
There's no Above and no Below.
That you are dead must be inferred,
And yet my thought rejects the word.

Twilight

So Mary died last night! To-day
    The news has travelled here.
And Robert died at Michaelmas,
    And Walter died last year.

I went at sunset up the lane,
    I lingered by the stile;
I saw the dusky fields that stretched
    Before me many a mile.

I leaned against the stile, and thought
    Of her whose soul had fled—
I knew that years on years must pass
    Or e'er I should be dead.

In September

The sky is silver-grey; the long
    Slow waves caress the shore.—
On such a day as this I have been glad,
    Who shall be glad no more.

The Promise of Sleep

Put the sweet thoughts from out thy mind,
The dreams from out thy breast;
No joy for thee—but thou shalt find
Thy rest

All day I could not work for woe,
    I could not work nor rest;
The trouble drove me to and fro,
    Like a leaf on the storm's breast.

Night came and saw my sorrow cease;
    Sleep in the chamber stole;
Peace crept about my limbs, and peace
    Fell on my stormy soul.

And now I think of only this,—
    How I again may woo
The gentle sleep—who promises
    That death is gentle too.

The Last Judgment

With beating heart and lagging feet,
Lord, I approach the Judgment-seat.
All bring hither the fruits of toil,
Measures of wheat and measures of oil;

Gold and jewels and precious wine;
No hands bare like these hands of mine.
The treasure I have nor weighs nor gleams:
Lord, I can bring you only dreams.

In days of spring, when my blood ran high,
I lay in the grass and looked at the sky,
And dreamed that my love lay by my side —
My love was false, and then she died.

All the heat of the summer through,
I dreamed she lived, that her heart was true
Throughout the hours of the day I slept,
But woke in the night, at times, and wept.

The nights and days, they went and came,
I lay in shadow and dreamed of fame;
And heard men passing the lonely place,
Who marked me not and my hidden face.

My strength waxed faint, my hair grew grey;
Nothing but dreams by night and day.
Some men sicken, with wine and food;
I starved on dreams, and found them good.

    *   *   *   *

This is the tale I have to tell—
Show the fellow the way to hell.

The Lost Friend

The people take the thing of course,
They marvel not to see
This strange, unnatural divorce
Betwixt delight and me.

I know the face of sorrow, and I know
Her voice with all its varied cadences;
Which way she turns and treads; how at her ease
Things fit her dreary largess to bestow.

Where sorrow long abides, some be that grow
To hold her dear, but I am not of these;
Joy is my friend, not sorrow; by strange seas,
In some far land we wandered, long ago.

O faith, long tried, that knows no faltering!
O vanished treasure of her hands and face!—
Beloved—to whose memory I cling,
Unmoved within my heart she holds her place.

And never shall I hail that other "friend,"
Who yet shall dog my footsteps to the end.

Cambridge in the Long

Where drowsy sound of college-chimes
  Across the air is blown,
And drowsy fragrance of the limes,
  I lie and dream alone.

A dazzling radiance reigns o'er all—
  O'er gardens densely green,
O'er old grey bridges and the small,
  Slow flood which slides between.

This is the place; it is not strange,
  But known of old and dear.—
What went I forth to seek? The change
  Is mine; why am I here?

Alas, in vain I turned away,
  I fled the town in vain;
The strenuous life of yesterday
  Calleth me back again.

And was it peace I came to seek?
  Yet here, where memories throng,
Ev'n here, I know the past is weak,
  I know the present strong.

This drowsy fragrance, silent heat,
    Suit not my present mind,
Whose eager thought goes out to meet
    The life it left behind.

Spirit with sky to change; such hope,
    An idle one we know;
Unship the oars, make loose the rope,
    Push off the boat and go...

Ah, would what binds me could have been
    Thus loosened at a touch!
This pain of living is too keen,
    Of loving, is too much.

To Vernon Lee

On Bellosguardo, when the year was young,
We wandered, seeking for the daffodil
And dark anemone, whose purples fill
The peasant's plot, between the corn-shoots sprung.

Over the grey, low wall the olive flung
Her deeper greyness; far off, hill on hill
Sloped to the sky, which, pearly-pale and still,
Above the large and luminous landscape hung.

A snowy blackthorn flowered beyond my reach;
You broke a branch and gave it to me there;
I found for you a scarlet blossom rare.

Thereby ran on of Art and Life our speech;
And of the gifts the gods had given to each—
Hope unto you, and unto me Despair.

The Old Poet

I will be glad because it is the Spring;
 I will forget the winter in my heart—
Dead hopes and withered promise; and will wring
 A little joy from life ere life depart.

For spendthrift youth with passion-blinded eyes,
 Stays not to see how woods and fields are bright;
He hears the phantom voices call, he flies
 Upon the track of some unknown delight.

To him the tender glory of the May,
 White wonder of the blossom, and the clear,
Soft green leaves that opened yesterday,
 This only say: Forward, my friend, not here!

They breathe no other messages than this,
 They have no other meaning for his heart;
Unto his troubled sense they tell of bliss,
 Which make, themselves, of bliss the better part.

Yea, joy is near him, tho' he does not know;
 Her unregarded shape is at his side,
Her unheard voice is whispering clear and low,
 Whom, resting never, seeks he far and wide.

So once it was with us, my heart! To-day
   We will be glad because the leaves are green,
Because the fields are fair and soft with May,
   Nor think on squandered springtimes that have been.

On the Wye in May

Now is the perfect moment of the year.
    Half naked branches, half a mist of green,
Vivid and delicate the slopes appear;
    The cool, soft air is neither fierce nor keen,

And in the temperate sun we feel no fear;
    Of all the hours which shall be and have been,
It is the briefest as it is most dear,
    It is the dearest as the shortest seen.

O it was best, belovèd, at the first.—
    Our hands met gently, and our meeting sight
Was steady; on our senses scarce had burst
    The faint, fresh fragrance of the new delight...

I seek that clime, unknown, without a name,
    Where first and best and last shall be the same.

Oh, is it Love?

O is it Love or is it Fame,
    This thing for which I sigh?
Or has it then no earthly name
    For men to call it by?

I know not what can ease my pains,
    Nor what it is I wish;
The passion at my heart-strings strains
    Like a tiger in a leash.

In the Nower

To J. De P.

Deep in the grass outstretched I lie,
    Motionless on the hill;
Above me is a cloudless sky,
    Around me all is still:

There is no breath, no sound, no stir,
    The drowsy peace to break:
I close my tired eyes—it were
    So simple not to wake.

The End of the Day

To B. T.

Dead-tired, dog-tired, as the vivid day
Fails and slackens and fades away.—
The sky that was so blue before
With sudden clouds is shrouded o'er.
Swiftly, stilly the mists uprise,
Till blurred and grey the landscape lies.

*   *   *   *

All day we have plied the oar; all day
Eager and keen have said our say
On life and death, on love and art,
On good or ill at Nature's heart.
Now, grown so tired, we scarce can lift
The lazy oars, but onward drift.
And the silence is only stirred
Here and there by a broken word.

*   *   *   *

O, sweeter far than strain and stress
Is the slow, creeping weariness.

And better far than thought I find
The drowsy blankness of the mind.
More than all joys of soul or sense
Is this divine indifference;
Where grief a shadow grows to be,
And peace a possibility.

At a Dinner Party

With fruit and flowers the board is deckt,
    The wine and laughter flow;
I'll not complain—could one expect
    So dull a world to know?

You look across the fruit and flowers,
    My glance your glances find.—
It is our secret, only ours,
    Since all the world is blind.

A Ballad of Religion and Marriage

Swept into limbo is the host
    Of heavenly angels, row on row;
The Father, Son, and Holy Ghost,
    Pale and defeated, rise and go.
The great Jehovah is laid low,
    Vanished his burning bush and rod—
Say, are we doomed to deeper woe?
    Shall marriage go the way of God?

Monogamous, still at our post,
    Reluctantly we undergo
Domestic round of boiled and roast,
    Yet deem the whole proceeding slow.
Daily the secret murmurs grow;
    We are no more content to plod
Along the beaten paths—and so
    Marriage must go the way of God.

Soon, before all men, each shall toast
    The seven strings unto his bow,
Like beacon fires along the coast,
    The flame of love shall glance and glow.

Nor let nor hindrance man shall know,
    From natal bath to funeral sod;
Perennial shall his pleasures flow
    When marriage goes the way of God.

Grant, in a million years at most,
    Folk shall be neither pairs nor odd—
Alas! we sha'n't be there to boast
    "Marriage has gone the way of God!"

THE EMPYREAN SERIES

---

about   The Empyrean Series is an imprint of Sublunary
         Editions, dedicated to producing new editions of
         overlooked works from the history of world literature.

editors   Jacob Siefring, Joshua Rothes

design   Joshua Rothes

web   sublunaryeditions.com/empyrean

etc   Empyrean Series titles are printed on acid-free, post-
         consumer paper.

THE EMPYREAN CATALOGUE